Latin
Crosswords

Latin
Crosswords

Professor Peter Jones
and
David Dare-Plumpton

Carroll & Graf Publishers, Inc. New York

Carroll & Graf Publishers, Inc.
19 West 21st Street
New York
NY 10010-0605

First published in the UK by Robinson Publishing 2000

ISBN 0–7867–0760–7

Printed and bound in the EU

Contents

Foreword

Plausus has done all the hard work constructing the puzzles. But he is used to it, being a retired Latin teacher and a compiler of crosswords for the London *Times* "Weekend Listener" and the *Sunday Telegraph*, and having won Best Crossword of the Year (1996) into the bargain.

Peter Jones, author of Barnes and Noble's best-selling *Learn Latin* and a simple-minded soul, has gasped in amazement at *Plausus*'s ingenuity, inserted the occasional joke, and added other material.

Peter Jones
Newcastle upon Tyne, UK

Plausus (David Dare-Plumpton)
Boston, UK

September 1999.

The Menu

Herewith for your entertainment and instruction a feast of fifty Latin Crosswords, all cruciverbally exquisite. They come dew-picked and farm-fresh in all shapes and sizes, tastes, tones, and textures, some rare, others well-done, some flambéd, others lightly tossed, some copiously drizzled in richly aromatic—and all the rest of the appalling drivel that passes for menu-talk these days. Well, at least it's pretentious.

Further, to perfect the experience, the puzzles have been tastefully arranged in order of difficulty into five courses, with ten succulent items in each course:

Course A: Soup – *Facillimum*   Course B: Fish – *Facilius*
Course C: Meat – *Facile*   Course D: Pudding – *Difficilius*
          Course E: Cheese – *Difficillimum*

Aids to digestion

1 Most important of all, an asterisk, *, indicates Latin. For example, 2.* means the answer to clue 2. is in Latin; "therefore*" would indicate you need the Latin for "therefore" to complete the clue.

2 A vitamin-enriched Glossary at the back provides hints for those really tricky Latin words or people you may have forgotten. But only to Sections A–D. When you are in Section E, you are on your own.

3 If a crossword is themed, its title may help with some of the clues.

4 Notes accompany the solution to each puzzle.

5 We have generally avoided cryptic clues.

6 Where a cryptic clue has been inserted to tickle the palate (about one clue in ten), the purpose is to offer a second, amusing, way into the answer. For example, we may write "I'm a small insect they love*". The answer is *amant* ("am ant", ho-ho). "Roman clothing* for a confused goat" would be *toga* ("confused" indicating that "goat" is an anagram). And, you will be appalled to hear, so on.

So watch out for:

(a) Lightly-done, exquisitely herbed **anagrams**, often signalled by words li]ke "perhaps", "possibly", "confused", "mixed" and so on. Thus: Daughter* I fail possibly = *filia*.

(b) Superbly fragrant **homophones**, signalled by a word of hearing, e.g. "You, we hear," would indicate "u".

(c) Gently grilled **reverses**, indicated by words like "up", e.g. "*Est*, if* up" = "is" (Latin "if" being *si*).

7 A "checked" square is one that, if it cannot be completed by a down clue, can be completed by an across clue (and vice versa). The crosswords are pretty thoroughly "checked", but where there are "unchecked" letters, we often give extra help (as you will see).

8 Latin U and V are regarded as interchangeable. Thus the "v" of the English answer "valetudinarianism" may form the u of a Latin word like *sum*.

9 There is an appendix on the pronunciation of Latin and the spelling of Greek (p. 150).

10 That's your lot. Now tuck in.

Course A: Soup *(Facillimum)*
A1 For starters

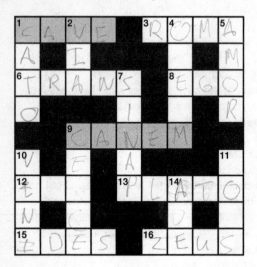

Clues Across

1.*/9.* Beware of the dog (4, 5)
3.* The Latin Eternal City (4)
6.* Across (5)
8.* I (3)
9. See 1ac
12. "Friends, Romans, countrymen—lend me an *aurem*" (3)
13. A philosopher with a stiff upper lip (5)
15. Beware of these, Julius! (4)
16.* The Greek Jupiter (4)

Clues Down

1.* A stern censor in ragged coat? (4)

2.* By way of (3)
4.* A small theatre—where Horace wrote 14, with hesitation? (5)
5.* Love in a backward Eternal City (4)
7.* A fold, bay or cavity behind the brain (5)
9. Her charms bewitched Odysseus/Ulysses (5)
10.* "_ _ _ _, *vidi*, *vici*" said Julius Caesar after the battle of Zela (4)
11. Shepherd loved by Galatea—a close relative, we hear (4)
14. Poem written by Horace (3)

A2 The missing number

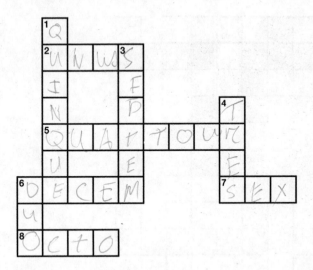

Review your Latin numbers one to ten. Peep below if you have forgotten them. Insert them so they fit into the diagram (they will fit only one way!). One of the numbers, however, is missing. Which is it?

Review for peepers: UNUS, DUO, TRES, QUATTUOR, QUINQUE, SEX, SEPTEM, OCTO, NOVEM, DECEM.

A3 Dem *ossa*, dem *ossa*

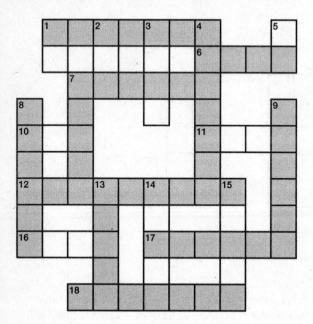

All the answers to the clues in shaded squares are BONES in Latin: *tibia, fibula, pelvis, patella, vertebrae, carpus, humerus, scapula, femur, calx, ulna, radius.*

Fit them in where they will go, with the help of these other clues.

Other clues

1.* These (m. pl.), or a greeting (2)
2.* 1,101 (3)
3.* The accused, but not sure? Possibly (4)
5.* Out of (2)
10. *Ulmus* (3)
14.* Berries or, we hear, Maenads (5)
15.* Bought female? (5)
16. The conspirators used their *pugiones* to do this to Caesar (4)

A4 Proverbs I

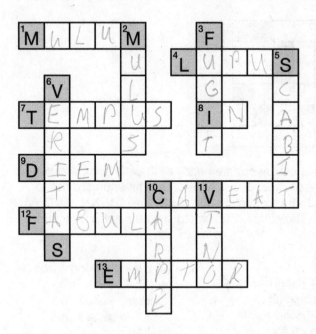

Here are six well-known English proverbs, all mixed up. First, unscramble them:

Talk of the / the blind / seize / truth / Devil / the day / leading / beware / flies / in wine / let the / the blind / is / time / buyer

Each of them has a Latin equivalent, scrambled just as badly below:

fugit / veritas / in vino / mulum / carpe / caveat / mulus / emptor / in fabula / scabit / tempus / lupus / diem

Fit the Latin equivalents into the puzzle, wherever they will go.

A5 Your number's up

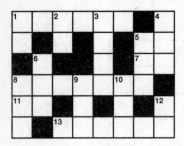

The **clues** in this crossword are nearly all in Latin numbers written out as words, e.g. *unus*, *duo*, *tres*, etc. But the **answers** to the crossword are to be written in Latin numerals—I, V, X, L, C, D, M and all that lot. Thus *duo* + *duo* would yield the answer (counts feverishly) IV.

Clues Across

1. $(novem)^3 + (quindecim)^2 +$ *(septem x sex)* (6)
5. $(decem)^3 +$ *quadraginta +* *(viginti ÷ duo)* (2)
7. *septem x quattuor –* *tredecim* (2)
8. *centum x quinque +* $(undecim)^2 + duo$ (7)
11. $(quinque)^3 + (quinque)^2$ (2)
13. *undecim x tres* (6)

Clues Down

1. *centum + unus* (2)
2. *viginti – novem* (2)
3. *(viginti + quattuor) ÷ tres* (4)
4. $(octo)^3 +$ *(undecim x quattuor) – unus* (3)
5. *mille + (triginta + tres ÷ tres)* (3)
6. $(novem)^3 –$ *(septem x undecim) – duo* (3)
8. *(viginti x viginti) +* *(quindecim x quindecim) +* *(quinque x quinque)* *x tres* (3)
9. *triginta – undecim* (3)
10. *(unus x unus) + unus +* *(unus x unus)* (3)
12. *duodecim ÷ duo* (2)

All done? Now—observe the collections of letters you have in the top two lines of the puzzle. There are twelve of them. At least nine English words can be made out of them. What are they?

Oooh! These puzzles! They're enough to make you 54 I 500!

A6 Zodiac filler

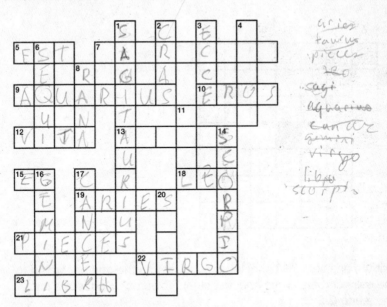

When you have solved the clues below, there will be gaps. You should be able to fill them in by completing the puzzle with the signs of the zodiac. If you cannot, wait till Pluto engages with Venus while Uranus is in the ascendant (when you will also find that Albert Einstein starts delivering your mail. Or is it a look-alike?).

2.* Tomorrow (4)
3.* Lo and behold! (4)
4.* A tree (5)
5.* He/she/it is (3)
6.* To follow (5)
8.* A frog (4)
10.* A god of love in Greek mythology (4)
11. *Viva voce?* (4)
12.* Life (4)
15.* *Exempli gratia* (abbrev.) (2)
20.* A cuttlefish tone in old photographs (5)

A7 The mink magpie

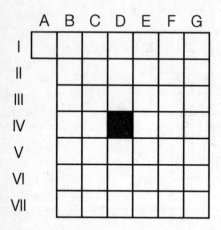

Put the answers (all Latin) letter by letter into the grid according to the cell numbers. Thus (the first clue) "Towards" = ad: put *a* into Bii, *d* into Cii.

When you have completed the grid, read clockwise from Ai—Gi, Gii—Gvii, Fvii—Bvii, Bvi—Bii, Cii—Fiii, Fiv—Fvi—Cvi, and so on in tighter and tighter circles, until you reach Dv.

By then you will have found seven Latin words that make up a well-known list. The eighth, which is hinted at in the crossword's title, is to be discovered.

Clues to Latin words
2 letters
Towards [Bii, Cii]; If [Gvii, Evii]; 45 [Gv, Dvii]; 99 [Dii, Eiv
3 letters
Thing [Cvi, Dvi, Bvii]; Goddess [Diii, Civ, Bv]; Through [Fiv, Giii, Giv]
4 letters
Boy [Evi, Fvi, Fii, Cvi]; Without [Fiii, Eiii, Bvi, Cvii]; Before, in front of [Fv, Ciii, Biii, Fii]
5 letters
We are [Gi, Fi, Fvii, Gvi, Dv]; Wine [Eii, Di, Ei, Biv, Ci]; Measure/method [Cv, Bi, Ai, Ev, Gii]

A8 State mottoes

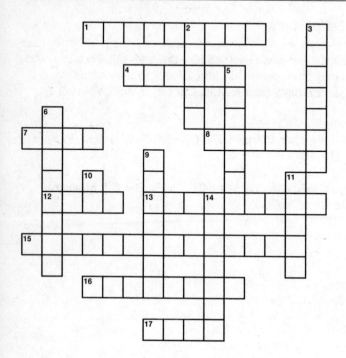

The following seven states of the U.S.A. all have Latin mottoes.
When you have completed the crossword, fill in the mottoes by
referring to the answers. Thus Alabama's motto will be found by
filling in the answers to clues numbered 5, 17, 4 and 1.

ALABAMA _ _ _ _ _ _ _ _ / _ _ _ _ / _ _ _ _ _ _ / _ _ _ _ _ _ _ _ 5/17/4/1
ARIZONA _ _ _ _ _ / _ _ _ _ 2/7
ARKANSAS _ _ _ _ _ _ _ / _ _ _ _ _ _ _ _ 8/9
IDAHO _ _ _ _ / _ _ _ _ _ _ _ _ _ 12/6
KANSAS _ _ / _ _ _ _ _ / _ _ _ / _ _ _ _ _ _ 14/13
MARYLAND _ _ _ _ _ _ _ _ / _ _ / _ _ _ _ _ _ _ _ _ _ _ _ 16/10/15
MISSISSIPPI _ _ _ _ _ _ _ / _ _ / _ _ _ _ _ 3/10/11

Clues

Note: the English, in lower case, translates the Latin in upper case italic—but the Latin has been scrambled! Work out the Latin, and insert that into the crossword. For example, no. 1 should be unscrambled to make *DEFENDERE*.

1. To defend = *END REEFED* (9)
2. He/she enriches = *TAD—IT* (5)
3. By valor = *UTTER VI* (7)
4. Our (f.) = *NO RATS* (6)
5. We dare = *A SUM DUE* (7)
6. Forever (f.) = *REPEAT UP* (8)
7. God = *SUED* (4)
8. He/she rules = *GARNET* (6)
9. The people = *SOUL PUP* (7)
10. And = *TE* (2)
11. By arms = *I, MARS* (5)
12. May she live/be = *TOES* (4)
13. Through difficulties = *PAPERS ARE* (3, 6)
14. To the stars = *A SAD RAT* (2, 5)
15. Multiply! = *I PANT, I'M ILL, I'M...UC...* (14)
16. Increase! = *ICE CREST* (8)
17. Rights = *U AIR* (4)

A9 Phrases and quotations

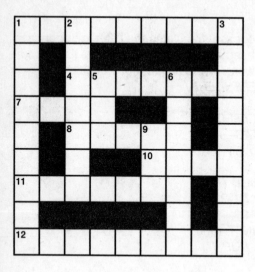

Clues Across

1.*/7.* The motto of the United States—one out of more (1, 8, 4)

4. See 10

7. See 1ac

8. Robbie, the mechanical man (5)

10.*/4.* Complicated Greek plays sometimes end with a god like 8 _ _ _ _ ex _ _ _ _ _ _ _ (4, 7)

11. Romans would have called the top floor of this house very *superior* and put airs on! (7)

12. Out of office? No, in it—because of good service (2, 7)

Clues Down

1.* Caesar's last words ? (2, 2, 5)

2.* Ghosts of the Roman dead—or monkeys! (7)

3.* This very old rock group hates change! (6, 3)

5. See 9

6. Confused critic, 'e is jaundiced, according to Pliny (7)

9.*/5.* "I hate and I love" said Catullus, in Latin " _ _ _ et _ _ _ " (3, 3)

A10 Abbreviations

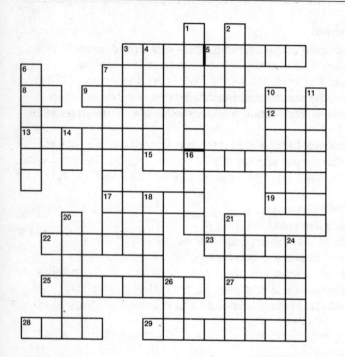

The clues to this crossword come in two sections. Ordinary Clues, which are, well, just ordinary (do these first), and Abbreviations which are, well, abbreviations—as you will see.

Ordinary clues

3. Therefore* backwards—a man-eating monster (4)
12. *Remus* in English—useful in a row! (3)
16.* Moon (crazy, man, with a tic!) (4)
17. To do with the city* (5)
19. "Virile" comes from Latin meaning someone who is a —what? (3)
24. *Tempestas* in English—you might kick one up (5)
27.* I trust a loyal dog (4)

Abbreviations

Now we get clever. The clues here take the form of sentences which involve a Latin abbreviation. You must identify the abbreviation and write it out in full, *wherever the words will fit in the crossword* (do not expect abbreviations of more than one word to appear together on the same line). One abbreviated word is used twice.

For example, you might find a clue using *i.e.*—you would then need to fill in *id* and *est* in the crossword wherever the words would fit.

a. The alcoholic, suffering a bad attack of the **d.t.**'s, blew kisses at the pink elephant (8, 7)

b. The coroner ordered a **p.m.** to be carried out on the cadaver—a stiff examination! (4, 6)

c. Because his **m.o.** was well known to the cops, the criminal was soon picked up (5, 8)

d. If you forget your lines, just **ad lib.** till the prompt wakes up (2, 7)

e. On the medicine bottle she read "Take twice a day—**b.i.d.**" (3, 2, 3)

f. Try and learn a foreign language, **e.g.** Latin! (7, 6)

g. No two epic poets are alike—**cf.** Homer and Virgil (6)

h. The Roman empire in the West lasted **c.** 600 years (5)

i. The penitentiary Governor received an ***hab. cor.*** from the judge for the felon's court appearance (6, 6)

j. **N.b.** Latin can seriously improve your health (4, 4)

k. Case adjourned **s.d.** to await reports on the man who thought subjects went into the genitive (4, 3)

l. Only at election time do the politicians care anything for the ***vox pop.***—though it never worried Pop (3, 6)

m. Turn to your text of Horace, p. 1 **ff.** (6)

n. Today you will learn all the cases—nominative, vocative, **etc.** (2, 6)

Course B: Fish *(Facilius)*

B1 All in Latin

The answers to this crossword are all in Latin—with just a few exceptions

Clues Across

1.* Sun (3)
3.* Winds (5)
6.* Tomorrow (4)
8.* Doctor (7)
10.* He/she stands (4)
13.* Countryside (3)
14.* You (s.) (2)
15. *iter* in English, or a stumble (4)
18.* Mythical *equus volans* (7)
19.* Roam about with a branch (4)
21.* 49 (2)
22.* 56 (3)
24. In English, I'm willing, I Cain, and I'm _ _ _ _ (4)
26.* He/she works (7)
27.* Underworld river where you might meet Charon (4)
28.* Snow (5)
29.* Road (3)

Clues Down

1.* Rocks (4)
2.* Bone (2)
4.* Letter (8)
5.* Bulls (5)
6., 17. The heavenly *gemini* (6, 6)
7.* Tacitus wrote a history of this country (gen. s.) (9)
9.* God willing (abbrev.) (2)
11.* You (s.) (2)
12.* Teachers about the gods (8)
16. Rupees (in English, abbrev.) (2)
17. See 6
18.* *Post meridiem* (abbrev.) (2)
20.* I have loved (5)
21.* *Id est* (abbrev.) (2)
23.* *Victoria regina* (abbrev.) (2)
25. I come after alpha (Greek!) (4)
27.* If (2)

B2 Prof's palindrome

Greeks and Romans loved palindromes (Greek *palindromos*, "running back again"). Here is one quoted by the Roman professor of education Quintilian (first century AD). Solve the crossword to complete it—it's very romantic. Aha, solvers of A1 will at once say, smelling a *rattus*: *Roma, amor...*

There is another small *rattus*: the answers that will solve the crossword are not clued. Those answers have to be discovered by answering the clues to the rest of the crossword.

For example, the first word of the palindrome is 1d. That will be found by answering 1ac, 9ac and 11ac. Ah, you ask, what about the second letter? Ah, we reply, this is a palindrome, so 1d should be matched by the last word you need, 17...

_ _ _ _ , / _ _ _ _ / _ _ _ _ _ _ _ / _ _ _ _ _ _ _ / _ _ _ _ / _ _ _
(1d, 7, 8, 9, 12, 17)

Clues Across

1. *Aries* (3)
4.* Gods (3)
6.* He/she is able (6)
11.* In another place (5)
14.* Ox, cow, or even a kind of turbot (3)
15. Greek goddess of disaster took food (3)
16.* You (s.) are (2)

Clues Down

2.* Belonging to the Sun God (Phoebus) or Moon shot! (7)
3.* "Having been moved" (m. pl.) (4)
4.* About or down from a bottomless goddess! (2)
5. *Id est*, briefly (3)
10.* I shall drink (5)
13.* Three times (3)
14. *esse* (2)

B3 Furry white stickers

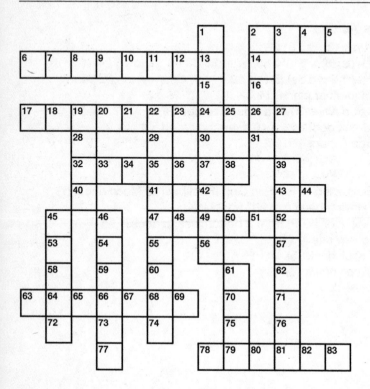

This crossword is to be filled in single letter by single letter. When it is completed, arrange as follows into a poem (*all* the answers are in Latin):

2ac/45d
Repeat
19d/32ac
Repeat
1d/22d/63ac
47ac/43ac/39d/78ac
6ac/17ac/61d
2d/46d

Clues

2 Letters: You (s.) **81 79**; By, from **9 10**; If **75 76**; 101 **23 16**

3 Letters: Road **61 70 68**; With **20 33 46**; Who **15 24 41**;
Thing **3 4 5**; But **52 43 39**; Countryside **59 54 17**;
Through **18 19 82**; 1200 **27 28 32**

4 Letters: Wave **30 37 50 51**; Worn by a Roman **21 83 29 44**;
Sea **31 22 8 40**

5 Letters: Thousand **65 66 25 80 74**; Place **60 55 47 53 72**;
Wall (acc.) **77 73 58 71 45**

6 Letters: Iron **63 64 34 35 36 69**; Crab (constellation) **62 48 67
78 57 82**; Turtle dove **42 49 56 38 26 14**

7 Letters: Soldiers **6 7 12 11 2 13 1**

B4 State mottoes II

Within this crossword you will find the Latin mottoes of four U.S. states: Maine, Michigan, New Mexico and North Carolina.

MAINE _ _ _ _ _ _ _ 25ac.
MICHIGAN _ _ 31 / _ _ _ _ _ _ _ _ 32 / _ _ _ _ _ _ _ _ _ _ _ 38 / _ _ _ _
_ _ _ 20 / _ _ _ _ _ _ _ _ _ _ _ 1ac.
NEW MEXICO _ _ _ _ _ _ _ 1d. / _ _ _ _ _ 12
NORTH CAROLINA _ _ _ _ 30 / _ _ _ _ 13 / _ _ _ _ _ _ 21

The mottoes themselves are not clued: you will have to work them out from the answers to the other clues. Here we introduce the concept of the "unchecked letter"—that is, a letter that cannot be derived from the other answers. Look, for example, at 1ac. It is not clued, because it is required for Michigan's motto. At the same time, you can see that the second and eighth letters cannot be gleaned from other clues. These, then, are "unchecked" letters.

Feeling merciful, we can reveal that 1ac's unchecked letters are I and P. Here is another tip. If you take all the unchecked letters in the crossword (including 1ac), they make the sentence OPEN AIR VIA THE US.

There! Aren't we generous? That's enough massaging. Now it's up to you.

Clues Across

10. Weird fearsome place, we hear, for an *aquila* to nest (5)
11.* *Magnus, maior,* _ _ _ (abbrev.) (3)
15.* Catullus' cockney dropping aitches (6)
17.* Famous Roman censor (4)
18.* Greater things (n. pl.) (6)
22 . *Avunculus* _ _ _ = USA (3)
23. Territorial Army (abbrev.) (2)
28.* Run together (s.)! vowels/syllables in poetry (5)
34.* *Rus* _ _ *urbe* (2)
35.* Well done! Bravo! 50% of cheers! (2)
36.* Wild irate Alpine people between Italy and Germany (5)

Clues Down

2.* She's reborn (6)
3.* By a cedar tree roughly cored (5)
4.* "I am burnt up" with love said Catullus (4)
5.* *Da* _ _ *basia mille* (2)
6.* Tribe living by the Seine partly troubled by queasiness (7)
7.* Irma's low down losing right (3)
8.* Take a picture with *this* of arched roof (6)
9.* *Deus* _ _ *machina* (2)
14.* Having used (m. pl.) (3)
16.* 999 (2)
19.* Having hated (acc. pl. m.) two bones!! (4)
24.* _ _ _ _ _ *m memento ... servare mentem* (Horace) (5)
25.* Another name for the island of Naxos, or Greek prefix "through" (3)
26. *Iterum cucurrit* (5)
27.* With a movement of the hand (5)
29.* Metallic element named after Latin for Paris (abbrev.) (2)
33. More than one *id est* (abbrev.) (3)
35. Abbreviation for Latin letter (2)
37.* 49 (2)

B5 Gods and goddesses

Clues Across

1. Belonging to the king of the gods (5)
4.* Bones (4)
7.* "We...?" (5)
8.* Places, and mathematical terms as well (4)
9. *Stella* is a _ _ _ _ in Latin (4)
11. Eros in Greek, but who in Latin? (5)
12. She was dragged off by Hades to the underworld (10)
16. ...the Roman underworld (5)
17. The words of a book, from the Latin "to weave" (4)
20.* A Latin goddess who is the goods! (4)
21. Goddess of harvests and corn (5)
22.* Hope this is Latin (4)
23. There were nine of them, me thinks! (5)

Clues Down

1. Two-faced god of the door seen at New Year? (5)
2. A virgin to guard the sacred hearth (5)
3.* ...with 22ac (3)
5. A sting in the tail for one born at the end of October (7)
6. Abandoned by Theseus on Naxos (7)
10. Only this bit of Achilles' foot was dipped in the Styx (3)
11. On the top of your *caput*! (3)
12. Another name for Apollo ("bright sun god" in Greek) (7)
13. Re scene—review and criticise (7)
14. So e's up at dawn in Greek... (3)
15.* ...after the night in Latin (3)
18.* The south-east wind—are you soundly sure? (5)
19. These give you *ebur* from *elephanti* (5)
21.* *Summa* _ _ _ *laude* (3)

B6 *Taberna rustica*

The Latin words in the shaded squares form an inscription in the dining-room of a country inn (*taberna rustica*). Write them out here and ponder their meaning:

_ _ _ / _ _ _ _ _ / _ _ _ _ _ / _ _ _ _ _ / _ _ _ _ _ _ _ / _ _ _ _ _ _

Hmm; pretty deep stuff. Yes. Undoubtedly. On the other hand, you could try writing the words out in the same order but with the letters divided up differently, as here:

_ / _ _ _ _ _ / _ / _ _ _ / _ _ _ / _ _ _/ _ / _ / _ _ _ _ / _ _ _ _ _ / _ _ / _ _ _ / _ _ !

Clues Across

1. What a *pudor*, nearly—it's bogus (4)
5.* By mouth (3)
8.* He/she will stand (6)
9. *Bos* (2)
10.* Three (3)
11.* To be driven/done/passed—silver one (3)
12.* Brave (6)
15.* Flourished (abbrev.) (2)
16.* Beware of the *antrum* (4)
19. *Crus* (3)
21.* He/she drinks (5)
22.* To plough (5)
24.* May it be pleasing (fut. imperative) (7)
26.* It remains/is left (6)
27.* If (2)

Clues Down

1.* Sh! (2)
2.* Old musical *capilli*! (4)
3.* Go away! (pl.) (5)
4.* 1,003 (4)
6.* I have asked (6)
7.* Go out! (s.) (3)
8.* I puff up, or swell with rage—soul *fortissimo*, perhaps (6)
13. You shout this when you see a *taurus Hispanicus* (3)
14.* He/she might know of the subjunctive? (6)
17. Aid and _ _ _ _ —on the Greens in the Circus Maximus? (4)
18.* And (2)
20. Guys and *puellae* ? (4)
21.* Berry, olive, fruit, pearl (4)
23. *Rattus* (3)
24. Sport for Peru (2)
25.* Bone (2)

B7 *Aquila musca*: Flying high

When you have finished this little crossword you will find that the shaded areas spell out a Latin proverb. As usual, the words of the proverb have to be constructed from answers to the other clues. Watch out for "unchecked" letters (see B4).

Clues Across

3.* They (nom. pl. m.) have been taken from their own country (9)
10.* Farmer (acc. s.) or famous soldier/governor (9)
11. Royal *navis* (abbrev.) (2)
12.* Pray (s.)! (3)
14.* With frost (4)
15.* You (pl.) illegally take over (9)
17.* Four (2)
19.* He may give (3)
22.* 600 (2)
24.* _ _ _ _ Porsenna, King of Etruria (4)
26.* Hallways (5)
27.* Gamblers (9)
29.* Roman State (abl. s.) (9)

Clues Down

1. Gallic *ater* or *niger* (4)
2. *Balaena ferox* (3)
3.* Give (s.)! (2)
4.* You lack, need (s.) (4)
5. *Superbus* like Tarquinius (5)
6.* Roman dress (4)
7.* Feed! Nurture! (On this alcoholic beverage?) (3)
8.* With such ankles of knucklebone dice (4)
9.* We go at the very bottom (m. s.) (4)
11.* Who (pl.)? (3)
13.* Suitable or attached (f. s.) (4)
16.* For a tower (dat. s.) (5)
18.* Farewell (s.)! (4)
20. Biblical *homo hirsutus* (4)
21.* I stand (3)
22.* By day (abl. s.), expire (3)
23.* Cottage/hut (4)
24.* Household god (3)
25. Abbreviation for 29 (3)
28. A type of *pestilentia* (abbrev.) (2)

B8 State mottoes III

Complete the crossword and key in the U.S. state mottoes by reference to the answer numbers shown. As before, the words required to complete the mottoes are unclued, and there are a few unchecked letters too (see B4). 14 could do with an L and E, for example; a couple of Ns will help out 27; 10d will benefit from S and I.

COLORADO _ _ _ 8 / _ _ _ _ 30 / _ _ _ _ _ _ 16
CONNECTICUT _ _ _ 4ac. / _ _ _ _ _ _ _ _ _ _ 10d. / _ _ _ _ _ _ _ _ 24d.
MASSACHUSETTS _ _ _ _ 1d. / _ _ _ _ _ _ 6 / _ _ _ _ _ _ _ _ _ 23d. /
_ _ _ 33 / _ _ _ _ _ _ _ _ _ _ 14 / _ _ _ _ _ _ _ 4d.
NEW YORK _ _ _ _ _ _ _ _ 52
WEST VIRGINIA _ _ _ _ _ _ _ _ 27 / _ _ _ _ _ _ 24ac. / _ _ _ _ _ _ 38

xxxvi

Clues Across

1. Tides *recedunt* and flow (3)
9. Ancient city—sounds hesitant! (2)
10.* With you (5)
13. Señor (abbrev.) or strontium (2)
15. Poetic *oculi* (3)
17.* You are (s.) (2)
18. I dry clothes or provide fresh *aer*! (5)
19. New wine, elephant's frenzy or a gerundive! (4)
21.* Before (4)
22. Long-player (abbrev.) (2)
26.* One of the Spice Girls is a honey (3)
34.* Thus (and ill, we hear) (3)
36. _ _ _ _ _ _ and Louise in the movie (6)
40. *Est* (2)
41. Very *siccus* (4)
42.* (S)he swims (5)
45.* "Without an age" abbreviated (2)
46.* I buy (3)
48.* Seen on tombstones in English as well (1, 1, 1)
49.* There (3)
51. *Ad* (2)

Clues Down

2. Two banks of oars on this *navis* (6)
3. Barrel in short (2)
5.* City (4)
7. Unable to *loqui* (4)
11. *Cura* (4)
12. Confused in the matter of* honey*, a film actress linked with Titania (5)
20.* Without offspring (abbrev.) (2)
25.* "On the right hand page" (abbrev.) (2)
26.* Poor man—half unhappy, too (5)
28. Nova Scotia in a nano-second (2)
29.* Go away! (s.) (3)
31. Jesus in Greek capitals (abbrev.) (3)
32. Lean over to reach French spirit* (4)
35. Goddess of the rainbow (4)
37. To our ears an ancient clown's trick (5)
39. Walt Disney's *cervus* (5)
43.* Citadel (3)
44. *Simia* that was King Kong (3)
47. "Just a sec.!"—Missouri (2)
49. Isaiah in Iceland (2)
50.* Cry of joy or despair (2)

B9 Shades in Hades

The answers to the clues in the shaded squares are all connected with the title of the crossword.

The *across* clues in **BOLD CAPITALS** are all anagrams.

The *down* clues in **BOLD CAPITALS** are "letter mixes". That means that the word, as well as being hinted at by the clue, is also hidden, letters jumbled, in the words of the clue itself. But not just anywhere: the first letter of the word you are seeking *begins* or *ends* one of the words in the clue, and the jumbled letters cluster round.

Example: let us pretend the answer to a letter-mix is "Hades". The clue might contain the words "the dash", where "dash" ends with an H, or "case had", where "had" begins with an H, and the rest of the letters in "Hades" appear round it.

Other clues, you will be disappointed to hear, are normal.

Across
1. This flower **HE LET** die (5)
5. The difference between "Leo" and "Leto"? Negative (3)
8. Pat's mixed up the wire bugs (4)
12. Judge **A CAUSE** (6)
13.* 151 (3)
14. This judge **SHUT A HARD MAN** up (12)
18.* Buy (s.)! A musical award, we hear? (3)
20. *Ubi habitat porcus*? (3)
21.* And a Spielberg film (2)
22.* You know (s.) (4)
24.* I burn (3)
26.* Wing (3)
27. *Clavis* or *unguis* (4)
28. Short second-year student (4)
30. **OUST** this giant (4)
32. **SCOUR** 10d (5)
34. Gold (abbrev.) (2)
35. Does **SIN SEEM** avenged by me? (7)
36. **X (20 ACROSS)** for this flower (4)

Down
1.* _ _ _ _ _ *et penates*, the household gods (5)
2.* She (2)
3. Boston had a party with this *potio* (3)
4. Has death no dominion **HERE**? (5)
5.* To be counted (8)
6.* An example would be a *tibia* or *femur* (2)
7. Lust antagonized **HIM**? (8)
8. Vulture—lusty. It tears **ME** up (6)
9. Rower to reach no salvation **HERE** (7)
10. Top ultimata from **ME** (5)
11. Is 'Pushy' suitable name for **ME**? (8)
15. Teach every black art with **MY** help (6)
16.* *Ad _ _ sem*—down to the last dime (2)
17.* Javelin (5)
19. **THIS MAN** judges sin most severely (5)
23.* Speak (s.)! (3)
25. *Filius* (3)
29.* Enough! But not *sat* or *satis* (3)
31.* Reflexive (2)
33.* Sh! (2)

B10 Lightweight country god

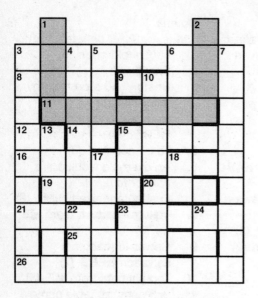

When this little crossword is complete you will find yourself faced with two further challenges:

i   Observe the three shaded (and *unclued*) answers at 1, 2 and 11. Fill them in in such a way as to make all three connected.
ii Then look at the whole completed grid. You should notice that it is unusual in one (alphabetical) respect. There is a cryptic hint in the title.

Clues Across

3.* After training squared up a horse, say (9)
8.* Wave (4)
9. *Magni aestimare*—to _ _ _ _ _ highly (5)
12. Greek letter *m* (2)
14. *Est* (2)
15. *Pugna* (5)
16.* Senatorial seats in the *theatrum*, but where Greeks danced or acted (9)
19. *Lacrima* or *scindere* (4)
20. *Votum* (3)
21.* After the manner of a given ceremony (4)
23.* To follow (5)
25. *Tali* (6)
26.* A writer of epigrams, or a month for hostilities? (9)

Clues Down

3.* Why? Mom—BarBque collapses, losing centre (9)
4.* Attract (s.)! Unjustly claimed missing millions (6)
5. *Dies* (pl.) (4)
6. *Obturamentum* (4)
7.* A pint drunk—exits *ursa* (9)
10.* Bee (4)
13.* Nettle (6)
15.* Bring (s.)! Iron shortly (3)
17. *Frequentare*, e.g. Plautus' *Mostellaria* (5)
18. *Ad* (2)
20.* _ _ _ _ *dare*—to set sail (4)
22. *Pix* (3)
23. *Ire per nivem*? (3)
24.* Having used (m. pl.) (3)

Course C: Meat *(Facile)*
C1 Author! Author!

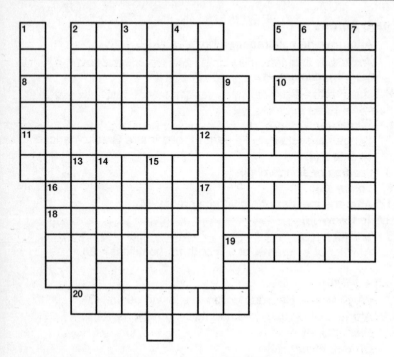

Here is one for literary experts—find the author.

First, fill in the clues below. Second, go to the "Author" clues, decide who each author is, and fit their names into the puzzle wherever they will go. One of the authors won't fit: he's your man.

Clues Across

5. A half-open *amphora* (4)
11. *auris* (3)
13. Latin egg-shaped Humpty-Dumpty (5)
17. *fidelis* (5)
19. *ita vero*—certainly denied in a muddle! (6)

Clues Down

1. A 16 which slaves rowed to the sound of a drum (6)
3. *ocelli* (4)
4.* Bird (4)
7. 2ac.'s Latin name may refer to this capital feature —heard deed, possibly (9)
16. *navis* (4)

Author clues

(A) I have kept the world chuckling with comedies like *Mostellaria* and *Miles Gloriosus,* and would have loved *A Funny Thing Happened...*

(B) I have tortured schoolboys ever since with my *Gallia est omnis divisa in partes tres*

(C) I wrote the *Histories of the Caesars*, whose exploits make our present leaders look a pretty pale lot

(D) I sighed over love poems for Lesbia, some of them featuring dead sparrows

(E) I was a great satirist, *panem et circenses* my best-known phrase

(F) I evangelised about how the cosmos was made in my *De Rerum Natura*—and helped the world discover atomic theory

(G) Sexy subjects like love (*Amores*) and *Metamorphoses* were my pleasure—and I spent my last years in exile for my pains

(H) I wrote odes, satires and epistles, and was close chums with Augustus and Virgil

(I) History was my subject—*Agricola, Annales* and *Historiae*—and "Romans make a desert and call it peace" my most famous saying

(J) I made endless speeches—*O tempora, o mores!* is one of my shorter utterances

(K) Sophisticated comedy was my scene, and *quot homines, tot sententiae* a famous saying of mine

(L) My *arma virumque cano* has sounded down the millennia

And the missing misfit is _ _ _ _ _ _ _ _

C2 *Ecce!* A palindrome

When you have completed this crossword, you will find a Latin palindrome running clockwise round the perimeter, beginning at IX 9. But since it is a palindrome, it also runs counter-clockwise round the perimeter, beginning at the same spot.

Fittingly enough, the palindrome is about circular movement —and fire. It can be filled in here:

_ _ / _ _ _ _ _ / _ _ _ _ / _ _ _ _ _ _ _ / _ _ / _ _ _ _ _ _ _ _ _ _ _ / _ _ _ _

Clues Across

B10* With wife (5); **B**11* Roman country God, protector of shepherds (4)

C12* Too late (4); **C**15 *cantavit* or Chinese dynasty pottery (AD 960—1279) (4)

D16* Barer, neuter (6); **D**18* 601 (3)

E19 Sacred syllable chanted (2); **E**20 Run together in Latin poetry (5); **E**21 *SPQR*, without the people? (2)

F22 Modern form of a *lectica*? (3); **F**24* *In curia cum _ _ _ _ _ _*, governing the Roman people (6)

G26* Belonging to you if male and singular (4); **G**28* I shall buy (4)

H29 A sea eagle (4); **H**30 Company for a short consul! (2); **H**31* To use (3)

Clues Down

ii2* Nine (2); **ii**13* Him (3); **ii**23* By ear (4)

iii3* They will bite (9)

iv4 Ancient city causes note of hesitancy (2); **iv**14 *olea* (4); **iv**27 Gallic dry (wine) (3)

v5* I am resting in peace (RIP) (9)

vi6 *Si*s and *sed*s—you need the first (3); **vi**17* 'He sends greetings' in two letters! (2); **vi**25 New lights, new signs— none about! (4)

vii7* "_ _ _ _ _ _ _ _ _ *igitur, iuvenes dum sumus*" (9)

viii8* Now (4); **viii**21* In position—U.S.A. and Trinidad & Tobago in a mix-up! (5)

C3 The missing emperor

The first century AD saw thirteen emperors in power in Rome. Some were considered Quite A Good Thing—like Augustus (the first emperor) and Titus (who finished building the Colosseum). Others were Villains of the Deepest Dye—like Caligula (who made his horse consul) and Domitian (who 'slit men's throats with a whisper'). Some did not last long—notably in AD 69, when after the death of Nero in AD 68 and the ensuing civil war, the imperial purple turned a bloody red and there were no fewer than four (Galba, Otho, Vitellius and finally Vespasian).

You will find all except one emperor (all clued by the dates of their reign) featuring in the clues below. Your task is to find the missing emperor!

[N.b. ** means they were assassinated.]

Clues Across
1. AD 69—79 (9)
5. AD 96—98 (5)
7. AD 69 (4)
9. *Fidus* _ _ _ _ _ _ _ , constant companion of Aeneas in Virgil's *Aeneid* (7)
12. AD 68—69** (5)
13.* Easy (6)
15.* Lambs (4)
16. AD 81—96** (8)
17.* Alas! (3)
18. 27 BC—AD 14 (8)
19.* _ _ _ _ *diurna*, Rome's daily paper nailed up in the Forum (4)

Clues Down
1.* Woe! (3)
2.* Dutiful (f.) (3)
3.* Alone (abl.) on the ground! (4)
4. AD 54—68 (4)
6. AD 69** (9)
8. AD 98—117 (6)
10. AD 41—54 (8)
11. AD 37—41** (8)
14. AD 79—81 (5)
17.* Sounds drunk here! (3)

C4 Whodunnit?

For this puzzle, you are a detective and have to find and highlight the guilty party lurking somewhere in the grid. On, then, with the false moustache and deer-stalker.

The clues to the person responsible are the answers to 1ac, 14ac., 8d. and 9d. *But, as you will find, there aren't any clues to these numbers.* Tricky, Watson, very tricky.

Also note: *across* clues are their normal merry selves, but we have added a little All-Latin help in square brackets. Thus, at 7ac, the first and second letters—i and ii—are formed by the Latin for "at, to", while the fifth and sixth—v and vi—are the Latin for "lest, so that not".

The *down* clues form word chains. This means that the last letter/letters of a word form the first letter/letters of the next word. Take 1d: "About" = C<u>A</u>; "Yes" = <u>AY</u>; "Muslim leader briefly" = A<u>YA</u> —and so on.

Clues Across

7.* Place next to (s.)! Serve a meal! Pan ode terribly! (6) [i, ii To, at*; v, vi Lest, so that...not*]

8. Lazy-y G.I.s flying for the period of full moon (8) [v, ii, vii, i Giant with 100 arms; vi, viii 49]

10. A *flumen* with *vada* would be *this* by men (8) [iii, iv, v Goddess*; ii, vi By, from*; vii 50]

11. *Catafractes* were *thus* protected (8) [I, iii, iv, vi Love*; i, viii To, at*]

12. USA state might briefly recall a *rostrum*? (8) [i, ii Lest*; iv, v, vi, viii Shaved*]

13.* Endless royal headband (6) [ii, iii, vi Now, already*; iv, v Down from*]

Clues Down

1. About / yes / Muslim leader briefly / *sunt* / *ruber* / data process

2. To, at* / cutting tool / zero day / 500 / 1000/ millibar / life [Greek]

3. E.g. *Sinon speculator* / *tu* in Bible/ I go* / pray* (s.)! / spoken

4. Wear* / gold* in short / United Arab (abbrev.)/ to* / 550*

5. *In* / part of a modern *calamus* / Brazil (abbrev.) / rupees/ *sive*

6. *verus* or *germaneus* / *cervesia* / Albanian *pecunia* / kilometre / 1010

C5 Howlers

Howlers are those terrible translations of simple Latin that occur only in examinations when fevered imaginations grasp at straws. Clues in **BOLD CAPITALS** are examples, in the shape of misunderstandings of popular sayings.

Clues Across

1.* These (m. pl.) sound a giggle (2)
2.* Beam of a cart; the Plough (Astronomy) (4)
5.* I crawl (5)
10.*/9.* **ITALIAN CAR WASH** (4, 3)
12.*/1d.* **INCLUDE THE WHITE WINE** (2, 3)
13.* Secretly shut mollusc (4)
15.* Terentius was one from this continent (4)
16.* For one in Higher Education? (3)
17.* Gold (abbrev.) (2)

I

18.* *auxilium* (3)
20.*/35.* **LOW COST AMERICAN FISH** (5, 4)
24.*/39.*/31d.*/22.* **BOTTOM TOO BIG FOR SLIGHTLY RIPPED SCOTTISH SHORTS** (3, 5, 4, 6)
26.* If* up (2)
30.* Four (2)
32.*/43.* **SWEAT SHOP FOR THE BOYS** (4, 4)
37.* On account of (2)
45.* Pan-pipes and ulcer (7)
47. *Tempta!* (3)
48.* For God (3)
50.* He/she buys (4)
51.* On account of (7)
52.* Aged (abbrev.) (2)

Clues Down

2.* Then (3)
3.* _ _ *cathedra*—from a chair of office (2)
4. Sounds like a bid from *him* to build a dyke in Wales (4)
5.* **CAR HIRE INFREQUENTLY AVAILABLE** (4, 4)
6.* _ _ *cetera*—and the rest (2)
8.* Opposite of *amo* for Catullus (3)

11.* *Id est* (abbrev.) (2)
14.* Animal's *cubilia* off rails? (5)
18.* Go away (s.)! (3)
19.*/29ac.* **BUM CLOTHING** (3, 5)
21.* In peace (4)
23.*/27ac.*/9.* **NOISY PEAK HOLIDAY PERIOD** (5, 3, 5)
25.* He/she stands (4)
30.* It (2)
33.*/28.*/7.* **I DO NOT WISH TO DANCE WITH THAT ITALIAN** (4, 2, 7)
34.*/1.*/51ac.*/1.* **AFTER THE WINE GOT HER UPRIGHT** (4, 3, 7, 3)
36.*/42.* **I TRAVELLED ON THE TRAIN AND FLEW FROM ITALY WITH THEM** (5, 4)
38.* Dunce; knave (4)
40.* For example, an *ulna* or *radius* (2)
41. *Gingiva* (3)
44. *Novum Eboracum* (abbrev.) (2)
45. *Homo delicatus* (3)
46. Consumed goddess of disaster (3)
48. *Medicus* (abbrev.) (2)
49.* I go there (2)

C6 Silver and gold

When you have completed the crossword, the Latin words in the shaded areas will set you a classical teaser.

If you don't know the answer, ponder the significance of the black squares and then let your eyes wander down the left–hand side of the puzzle, 1–48, and then down the right hand side, 13–38. Is it another terrible joke? You betcha.

Clues Across

1. Letter of Greek alphabet; a *suspirium*, we hear (3)
4.* Prayer, entreaty (4)
7.* I (3)
9.* Them (acc. pl. f.); you (s.) may go (3)
10.* Elms (4)
12.* You (s.) give (3)
14. Common Greek wine (7)
17.* I burn our mixture (3)
18. Belonging to the first lady in poetic twilights (4)
19.* One driven from his own country (4)
20. *Milites Americani* (3)
21.* I have ransomed (6)
23.* On right hand page (abb.) (2)
24.* But (3)
26.* He/she goes (2)
27.* To go (3)
29.* Love (s.)! (3)
30.* Death; murder (3)
31.* Man (3)
33.* Approach! Go to (s.)! (3)
35.* As; in order to (2)
37.* Short for *nisi* (2)
39.* Incense; perfume (3)
41.* 11 (2)
42.* For a long time (3)
43.* By eye (abl. s.) (5)
45.* With horses (abl. pl.) (5)
48. Rhode Island (abb.) (2)
49. Argon in Arkansas (abb.) (2)
50. Info (3)
51. *Ad* (2)

Clues Down

1.* Through (3)
2.* Fiercer (abl. s.) i.e. rave so wildly (8)
3.* That of yours (m. s.) (4)
4. Pet name for *feles*? (4)
5. Printer's measure or accusative ending? (2)
6.* 11 (2)
7.* I have brought up/out (5)
8.* Famous rotting Roman fish sauce (5)
11.* Books (5)
13.* Sun (3)
15. Negatives (4)
16.* In the room (abl. s.) (4)
18.* *Exempli gratia* (abb.) (2)
22.* Thus; so (3)
23. Same as 48ac (2)
25. Goliath's conqueror (5)
26.* 999 (2)
28.* Go out (s.)! (3)
30.* I swim (4)
32.* I have entered, gone in (5)
34.* For a leader to be led (4)
35.* Wife (4)
36. *Adliga!* (3)
38.* Law, justice; soup, broth (3)
40. 13d in English (3)
44. Musical note (2)
46.* *Quod erat* (abb.) (2)
47. One French article (2)

C7 Delay* not

Here you are hunting for a famous quotation and its author. The author runs down the shaded left hand side of the puzzle, the quotation across the shaded top and down the shaded right hand side.

23, 24 and 25 across provide an English hint—words contained in the title of a famous Beatles song!

The final catch: one word of the quotation is missing—though hinted at in the title of the puzzle. Fill it in here:

_ _ _ _ (4)

Clues Across

7.* I carry (4)
8. To make a mistake, rather like the Latin (3)
9.* Short-lived emperor (AD 69) (4)
10. Type of *boletus* for Claudius after writing his memoirs!? (6)
11. Once upon a time, perhaps aged 49* in *quem*? (6)
12. *Fasces* carried by the *lictors* (4)
14. He had Troy built, but cheated on his word (8)
16.* You would see jerks here all over Greece (8)
18.* Of hope for all studying Latin (4)
19.* Humorously (6)
21.* Beef (6)

Clues Down

1. You might see *sanguis* flowing here (4)
2.* Birthplace of Jason is wild—is cool (6)
3.* Once called Parthenope this New City was on a bay in Campania (8)
4. *Cornix* (4)
5. Greek violet—atomic weight 127, symbol I (6)
6.* Teddy-bear president is 'gift of God' in Greek (8)
13.* A bitter-sweet or sharp/foolish figure of speech (8)
15.* I walk/prowl around (8)
17 Belonging to the daughter of Tantalus—stony faced (6)
18.* This race of women is bane (no—a blessing!) to Romans (6)
20.* Horace's *tempus _ _ _ _ rerum* (4)
22.* Plague or medical pestilence (4)

C8 In Kansas

The story so far...

When a 16d hit her *fundus* in Kansas,1ac accompanied by 20ac met up with 12ac/ 5ac, 26ac (3, 7) and 31ac, and together they set off down the 8ac/12—45 (color this diagonal appropriately) *ut viderent* the 40ac/47ac in... But we will leave you to finish the grid at 48ac.

As usual, these answers are unclued and have to be reconstructed from the answers to other clues. There are some "unchecked" letters: you will appreciate, for example, L at 12, G and V at 26, and B at 16—and a few others we're keeping secret at the moment.

Clues Across

9.* Rust or envy (6)
19. Two letters expressing hesitation or acc. ending (2)
20.* *In _ _ _ _* : entirely (4)
22.* This (n.) (3)
24. *Deus Aegyptius solis* (2)
32. The Romans were (supposedly) famous for this sort of gory rave-up (4)
33. Written by Sheridan— *Aemuli* (6)
35.* In winter (5)
37.* *Solis _ _ _ _ _ _* : at sunset (6)
43.* Different; divided (f. s.) (8)
46.* 2000 (2)

Clues Down

2.* Sheep (4)
3. *Insula Rhodiensis* (abbrev.) (2)
4. *Vox populi, vox Dei* is an example of a Latin one (3)
5. *Gallina* (3)
6.* Mistresses (of the house) (4)
7.* Gold in short (2)
10. Leave quietly (4)
11.* Hunter and constellation (5)
13.* Now in the past (3)
14.* Your (dat. s.) (3)
17. New Testament (abbrev.) (2)
18. Negative (2)
21.* I was roasting (8)
23. *Diva* but at La Scala (6)
25.* In the hallways (abl. pl.) (6)
26.* To read (6)
27. Elizabeth *Regina* shows hesitation (2)
28.* Two (2)
29.* Anywhere (6)
31.* 105 (2)
34.* Triumphant cry (2)
35. Her Majesty (abbrev.) (2)
36. *Tabula* (3)
38.* 101 (2)
39.* I take up this type of wrestling (4)
41.* Anger (4)
42.* Delay 50 with silver (3)
44.* You (s.) (2)
45.* Coin (2)

C9 Proverbs II

The shaded squares contain six Latin proverbs, listed I—VI below. The numbers in square brackets after them refer to their English equivalents:

I 5d / 10 (7, 5) [= 4, 5, 4, 5]
II 37ac / 19 / 20 / 5ac (6, 5, 5, 6) [= 4, 6, 4, 3]
III 17 / 9 / 43 / 51 / 52 / 21 (3, 4, 4, 5, 5, 3) [= 3, 4, 8, 2, 3, 4]
IV 24ac / 27 / 15 (5, 7, 4) [= 4, 4, 4, 4, 4]
V 45 / 44 / 37d / 31ac / 44 (3, 3, 3, 4, 3) [= 1, 6, 2, 4, 2, 1, 6, 6]
VI 28 / 17 / 2 / 24d (5, 3, 5, 8,) [= 4, 5, 6, 2, 8]

Here are the English equivalents, but they have been jumbled:
Haste like a speed friend father; son that ends more well is

less in need; a friend that glitters is not all parsnips; fine all's well; words like no gold butter indeed. First unscramble these, then complete the crossword and match them to their Latin equivalents.

Aha! But wait! There is more fiendish cunning to come. When you have worked out the English proverbs, you can probably guess much of the Latin already. So the clues to the Latin words (numbers printed bold in the crossword) do contain the Latin, but its letters are scrambled up within the word(s) somewhere. For example, 2d "<u>untal</u>ented" hides letters that make up *alunt*. Ouch! But at least the letters all occur next to each other, even if scrambled.

Clues Across (*Clues Down on p. 60*)

1.* Battle where Hannibal was defeated (4)

5.* "Fusil" I found is the French for "gun" (6)

10.* I swam ten lengths (5)

12. Greek letters and* a small Roman coin* (4)

14. Old King of Pylos (6)

16.* 51 (2)

17.* On Neptune no life (3)

19.* The taper has burnt down (5)

21.* A very loud Greek was Stentor (3)

22.* What Socrates swallowed finally (6)

24.* I go out if it is fine (5)

25.* Milk (3)

28.* "Fortune favors the brave" (5)

31.* Catiline was a threat to Cicero (4)

32.* *Id est* (abbrev.) (2)

33.* "*Da _ _ basia mille*" (Catullus) or 1001! (2)

35. Julius gave his name to emperors like Wilhelm (6)

37.* Squalid tenements on the Subura (6)

39.* 200 (2)

40.* On the right hand side— *recto* (abbrev.) (2)

41. *Nos* in America? (2)

42. Muhammed *pugilis*? (3)

43.* "Status Quo" dance music (4)

45.* The usual suspects and their alibis (3)

46.* They have sprouted and grown out (n. pl.) (5)

48. *Ad* (2)

51.* I endorse it entirely (5)

52.* I have to drink—it's a rum urge (5)

53.* She's been seen showing passport endorsement (4)

C9 Proverbs II *(continued)*

Down

2.* An untalented amateur (5)
3.* *Ego* (acc.) (2)
4.* _ _ _ _ *Domini* (4)
5.* Vestal Virgins in a festival had honored seats (7)
6.* He/she had gone out irate (5)
7.* As, so (2)
8.* With salt (4)
9.* An ill omen (4)
11.* Reverse 7 in acc. (2)
13. Address *dominus* or *magister* thus? (3)
15.* Soup? (4)
18.* Bone (2)
20.* Coming last is no failure (5)
22.*/23.* = 202 (2,2)
24.* Does the Mafia limit membership? (8)

26.* Black male? (4)
27.* Can't roots grow in this soil? (7)
29.* His/hers (4)
30.* Defendant is female (3)
31.* Stork (7)
34. *Est, est—Dea Aegyptia*! (4)
36.* Sharpening (6)
37.* I question (3)
38. A place for experimental work* (no alternative) (3)
44.* Was a *murmillo* glad at the end of the show? (3)
47.* Three times (3)
48.* You see here the reverse of 7 (2)
49. *Sive* or *seu* or neither! (2)
50.* 4 (2)

C10 Rigorous limerick

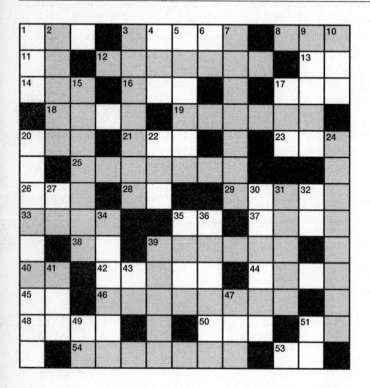

When the crossword is complete you will be able to astonish friends with a favorite old limerick (about a female Latvian equestrian and a large, contented feline) translated into Latin:

_ _ _ _ _ _ / _ _ _ _ _ _ _ _ _ / _ _ _ _ _ _ _
_ _ _ _ / _ _ _ _ _ _ _ / _ _ / _ _ _ _ _ / _ _ _ _ _ _ _
_ _ _ _ _ _ _ / _ _ _ _ _ _ _ _
_ _ _ _ _ _ _ / _ _ _ _ _ _ _
_ _ _ / _ _ _ _ _ _ / _ _ / _ _ _ _ _ / _ _ _ _ _ _ _

As usual, the words you need to complete the limerick are not clued, and there are some "unchecked" letters. These unchecked letters, taken together, make up "Ruler rents turban".

Clues Across

1.* So, thus (3)
3.* A flowering bush (acc. s. f.) (5)
11.* Down from, about (2)
13.* Which was (to be proved) —(abb.) (2)
14. I lose my way (and my *o* in Latin) (3)
16.* Force (acc. s.) goes with vigor (3)
17.* Her pigs!! (3)
18. *Date!* (4)
20. *caespes* (3)
21. _ _ _ Guevara (3)
23. Sort of talk you give to generate 16 (3)
26.* Beneath (3)
28. *Securis* or cleaver (2)
29.* I delay, slow down, hinder—road confused with junction? (5)
35.* In the matter of the Italian king (2)
37. A punch (4)
38.* You (acc. s.) (2)
42.* I trot roughly on one having been worn down (5)
44.* Then, tunic I forgot (4)
45. Italian river for Pluto first and last (2)
48. Trade/export from river at 45 (4)
50.* Goddess of Wealth; power, resource (3)
51. Egyptian sun-god (2)
53*. I give (2)

Clues Down

1. Caesar, beware of just one of these! (3)
2.* At the rear, thrice go (5)
4. Startled? Hullo! (1, 2)
5.* Always (6)
6.* By, from (2)
9.* Mares (5)
10*. Goddess (3)
17.* Without lawful issue (abb.) (3)
20.* A foot and a half sees quips flying wildly (9)
22. Put a spell on six in Greek (3)
27. Ulster Unionist (abb.) (2)
30.* You (pl.) are going away— a—is part of the whole (6)
32. *Defensor Fidei* (abb.) (2)
34. Greek measure—in place where I met Ron? (6)
35.* Duly, properly for the ceremony (4)
36.* I do not (3, 3)
41.* Night (3)
43. Rhode Island (abb.) (2)
47. Where you might take *aquae*, or what did for Cleopatra first to last (3)
48 Letter of Greek alphabet— tastes delicious! (2)
51. On the right hand page (abb.) (2)

Course D: Pudding *(Difficilius)*
D1 Birds, wasps, clouds, frogs

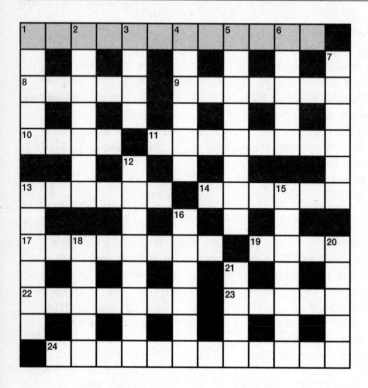

Clues Across

1. Greek comedian shapes ration oddly (12)
8. The actress Kelly is on first-name terms with gratitude in Latin (5)
9. Left on Naxos by Theseus—an operatic solo with sad end!? (7)
10. *navis* (4)
11.* To be taught in Latin (sounds like the quack will finish them off!!) (8)
13. Creates *silentium* (6)
14.* Juvenal's guard (to guard the guards) (6)
17.* "Let us sing" in Latin—unable to muse wildly? (8)
19. Beat it, *tympanista*! (4)
22. Horace's almost Socratic mountain (7)
23. Greek epic I laid apart (5)
24. Underworld judge—short *rex* possessed a chap *ita* (12)

Clues Down

1. Io's guardian, whose 100 eyes Hera transferred to the peacock's tail (5)
2. Father of Penelope—a too-high flyer with one added (7)
3.* In French very Latin number (4)
4. The Alexandrian wonder of the world to light you up! (6)
5. Murderer of Nero's mother is cute an' mixed up (8)
6. *Finem fecit—finis* editor in short (5)
7. Martial's gladiator and Greek god of travellers (6)
12. Use El Cid horribly—a member of an ancient Syrian dynasty (8)
13.* Not i.e., but this is (3, 3)
15. A pinkish delight of Anatolia? Sweetie! (7)
16. The nine would live happily here (6)
18. Whence Boreas blows (5)
20.* The Latin method or manner (5)
21. *leo* (4)

D2 Agnew's hope

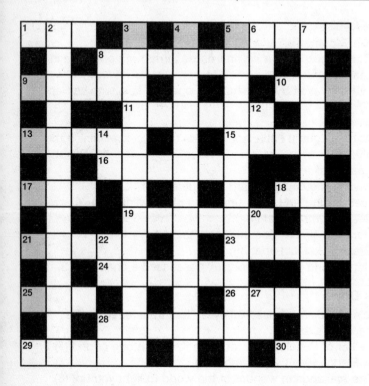

The shaded squares, when complete, will reveal a famous saying which could well have been the motto of the Agnew family.

Clues Across

1. Expensive dinner item according to Pliny—*glacies* in English (3)
5.* Breast, mummy (5)
8. A notoriously venal Roman judge possessing nothing, bulging like a bean or onion (7)
9. The lady with nine books, then six, then three... (5)
10. *Asinus* in English (3)

11. These long-tailed ones were seen flying at Caesar's funeral (6)
13. Badly equip—might cause *offensio* (5)
15. Take off one's *pilleum* (5)
16. An opening that might be limper, or a battle* without you, we hear, o! (6)
17. Electrically charged particle in Euripides' tragedy (3)
18. *Cerva* (3)
19.* They owe, ought (6)
21. *Fucus* is what the lady of pleasure puts on her cheeks (5)
23. *Potestas* (5)
24.* Inborn, inherent (f.) (6)
25. *Oleum* (3)
26. Vast beast known by its (Greek) nose-horn (5)
28. Each morning after her night's work Penelope had to _ _ _ _ _ _ _ the shroud (7)
29.* Even, too (5)
30. Cleopatra's chosen killer (3)

Clues Down

Now pay attention. The answers to 6, 8, 12, 14, 20, 22, 27 and 28 down, each consist of *two-letter words*, some English, some Latin. The clues to these are presented here in *alphabetical* order of *solution* (thus the "small Roman coin" begins with *a*).

Small Roman coin; via; *miles Americanus*; *ille*; *deus Aegyptius*; Latin tin (abbrev.); *ad*; *sursum aut supra*

Fit these in to the puzzle where they will go. To help you, the sixteen letters of these clues could be re-arranged into: Hang! Your asp bites!

Other clues down

2. Sherlock Holmes in ancient Rome? (13)
3.* Horace listened to his Lalage "_ _ _ _ _ / _ _ _ _ _ _ _ _" (5, 8)
4.* Latin directions to the hive and the honey-bees? (3, 3, 3, 4)
5.* "A lot in a little" (6, 2, 5)
7.* High Roman Catholic Service (5, 8)

D3 The Seven Hills of Rome

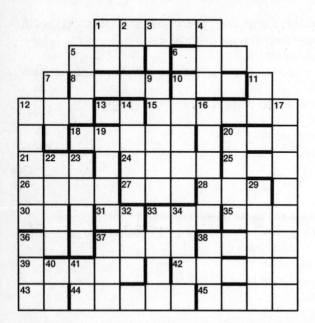

Rome was a city set on seven hills—the Aventine, Caelian, Capitoline, Esquiline, Palatine, Quirinal and Viminal. If you want a mnemonic for them, try "Can Queen Victoria Eat Cold Apple Pie?".

They are all hidden in this crossword—each one forming the shape of a hill, either with a sharp point ( ) or with a flat top ( ). Your job is to complete the crossword and then find and color in the hills, to make some Very Pretty Shapes. You could even do them all in different colors. Try to restrain your mounting excitement as you near the tops.

Clues Across

1.* To arise; to spring up (5)
5.* Alas! (3)
6. A waterfall, bringing back nothing* (3)
8.* Water (4)

10./23d. A brand of Caesar's Spanish drink (3, 4)
12.* Dispute or lawsuit leading to a 10 down (3)
13.* As much as you please (2)

15. 51* pitcher* needed to pass water here? (6)
18.* Of the sky (5)
20. New one? (3)
21. *Catulus* or *Canis Minor* (3)
24. Bufo, the sycophant (4)
25. Poetically all up with *remus*, we hear? (3)
26.* Of 27—the Spanish cry with one! (4)
27. *oleum* (3)
28.* Grape (3)
30. No French reply—if you please! (3)
31.* 51 (2)
33.* A place of higher education for one (3)
35. *Gladius* or *pilum*? (3)
36. A *societas* for nameless *ebriosi* (2)
37.* Threat—and a Greek coin (4)
38.* By the sword (4)
39.* Soft version of Caesar's first name (5)
42.* Sick, ill (5)
43.* 105—a summary of life (abbrev.) (2)
44. *Populus* in Colorado ski resort (5)
45. *Damnum*—can't take many more of these (4)

Clues Down

1. Old Etonian (abbrev.) (2)
2. *es-ne*, we hear? (2)
3.* *Duo* or I have gone (2)
4. *Tres* (3)
5.* *Habet* (3)
7.* Perish by day (3)
9. Greek double pipes (5)
10. See 12—mix up trail (5)
11. *idem ac* 36ac (2)
12.* Charm of hare with slight change—poles apart (5)
14. Mother of Apollo and Artemis, Latin Latona (4)
16.* To be put on, clothed in (5)
17. They used to make horses' harnesses from the Latin for "reins" (8)
19. A Latin nothing dye (4)
20.* A new star?! (4)
22.* Sedge, reed (4)
23. See 10ac (4)
29. Greek up-beats (opposite of *theses*) (5)
32.* For them—if one rises! (3)
33.* Ladies together as one! (4)
34. Type of *panis*, whichever way you look at it (4)
36. Accusative, or a double century (3)
37.* I am an up-and-coming mouse! (3)
38. *Anguilla* (3)
40. Authorised Version (2)
41. Iowa (2)

D4 Hanging by a thread

Clues Across
1. He found himself at the sharp end of the tyrant's way of life (8)
6.* Of account or weight in open site (5)
8.* May you keep up, maintain (like jams and pickles!) (9)
9.* Him (acc.) (3)
10. Funnily to us, _ _ _ _ and his chum Ephialtes were two mythical giants (4)
11.* Amazing the world—the _ _ _ _ _ _ mundi (6)
13. Tragedian, philosopher, millionaire and tutor to Nero— 'e canes wildly (6)
14. The wood or mountain where the centaurs dwell—oo help! (6)
17. River flowing in Thessaly quietly East-North-East to the States (6)
18. All the fun of the nundinae! (4)
20.*/23.* Horace's faithful bottle—the same age as consul Manlius (Odes xxi.i) (3, 5)
24.*/22.* Polyphemus (Aeneid iii 658) or Frankenstein—makes you shudder (8, 9)

Clues Down
1.* I keep on repeating (5)
2. Virgil known by his town of origin (7)
3.* I beget, bring into being (4)
4.* According to one's prayer (2, 4)
5.* The reply sounds like a goose (5)
6. The famous Lesbian poetess's real name (starts like the end of a letter!) (7)
7. Antigone's sister—she sounds like a lot (6)
12. Nymph changed by Apollo into a flower ... in its masculine form, found atop Corinthian capitals (7)
13.* It crawls (6)
15. Heroic (!) lover and swimmer (7)
16. Sheet of paper created by a Latin fourth (6)
17. "Quae pars?" asks the teacher when you do this to a word (5)
19.* To the capital (5)
21. Great god—the Egyptian canal's rising up (4)

D5 Slander at the opera

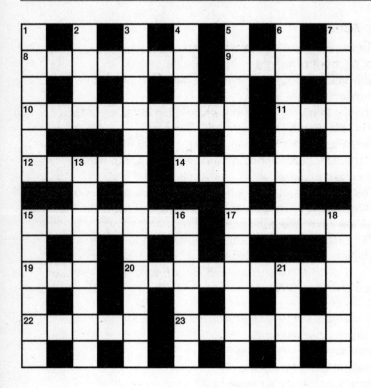

Clues Across
8.* To speak against, contradict (7)
9.* Sung works (5)
10. Litorally (!), in front of the Black Sea (9)
11.* Her (acc. s.) (3)
12.* Having been sown (nom. f. pl.) wild as tea (5)
14.* May you (s.) decide...to erect these? (7)
15. Sounds like more than one of the ribs in Greek over the lungs (7)
17. You give (pl.)* the name of Darius' general defeated at Marathon (5)
19. *Patior*—or serve again after it at tennis (3)
20.* To divide in the form of an X might cause reds' upheaval (9)
22.* They feed, nurture (5)
23. Delphi and Ammon were *so clear?!* (7)

Clues Down
1.* Body (6)
2. Muse of history—sounds like that Egyptian queen (4)
3.* "Don't trust that horse!" Laocoon warned the Trojans in *Aeneid* ii (4, 2, 7)
4.* Invented, made up (m.) (6)
5.* Horace's shining aqua-jet? (*Odes* 3.xiii) (4, 9)
6.* They desert (8)
7.* Trees, dates, hands, prizes (acc.) (6)
13.* Where Romans watched plays (8)
15. Common epithet for Athena (6)
16. He carried the *fasces* in ancient Rome, or sounds as if he ran his tongue over iron! (6)
18. Use ass roughly to get to the Campanian town of Aurunca (6)
21.* Hall, or emperor's court found in Gaul anywhere? (4)

D6 Enigma variations

You want terrible jokes? You got 'em.

Below is an enigma in the form of a question and answer. When you have completed the crossword, fill the blanks in with reference to the numbers of the clues provided.

Both question and answer are in Latin. Translate them. Geddit? No? I cannot say I am surprised. It is a seriously frightful joke. You will be mad when you read the explanation. Not for nothing are these called *cross*words. Cross? They're *livid*.

QUESTION: _ _ _ / _ _ _ _ _ _ / _ _ _ _ _ _ _ _ _ / _ _ / _ _ _ _ _ _ _ / _ _ _ _ _ _ _ _ _ _ / _ _ _ _ _ _ _ _ _ _ **??**
[1ac. / 4 / 12 / 13 / 15 / 16 / 22]

ANSWER: _ _ _ _ / _ _ _ _ / _ _ _ _ _ _ _ _ _ _ / _ _ _ _ _ _ _ **!!**
[25ac. / 30 / 39 / 42]

As usual, the words you need to complete the appalling joke are not clued: you have to find them by solving the other clues. There are some "unchecked" letters. 22ac, for example, would benefit from an L and two Us.

Clues Across TOP

9. Manuscript in Mississippi (2)
11. *Sive* in Oregon (2)
23. Note it's back (2)

Clues Down TOP

1. A *sestertius* is an example of a Roman _ _ _ _ (4)
2. For *cineres post mortem*? (3)
3. Roman Catholic (2)
4. Of a confused *agrestis*? (3)
5. A diva's crispy *panis coctus*—Dame Nellie?! (5, 5)
6. Non-specific urethritis (3)
7.* Her (acc.) or I may go (3)
8. *Magister Indus*—sir's angry (3)
9. List of food *in taberna*? (4)
10. More than one "anas" seems wild (5)
14. God willing (2)
17. Automobile Association (2)
18.* It [see 36] (2)
19.* Where? (3)
20. South Africa (2)
21. Quartermaster (abbrev.) (2)
22.* 50 (1)

Clues Across BOTTOM

29.* Water, in short (2)
34. Mater's lost her head— they show hesitation (3)
35.* To be hungry (7)
36. *Id est* [see 18] (2)
37.* 150 (2)
38.* Chewed-up goat worn by Romans (4)
41.* If (2)

Clues Down BOTTOM

24.* Eagle (6)
25. Short, clever, instant *ioci* (5)
26.* Shoulders (5)
27. Award for acting—*o cicatrix*! (5)
28.* I destroy (5)
31. *Flumen* in Spanish (3)
32. The hundred-eyed watcher of myth (5)
33. *Ludibrio habere* (5)
38. The beat of the *sol*? (3)
40.* 900 (2)

D7 Watch your pelvis

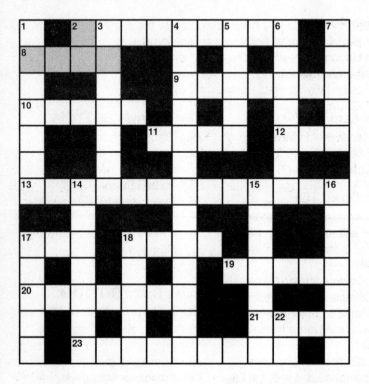

8ac and 2 down together form an English anagram of the hero of this puzzle. You might even recognise some of his songs in the clues...

Clues Across

2.* See 4 down (9)
8. Rugged isle, where the Olympic Games were organised (4)
9.* See 3 down (7)
10.* Sand, where gladiators fought (5)
11.* *ita*, *sic*, or Latin for incense (4)
13.* See 17 down
17. *gallina*—if it ate, you were lucky (3)
18.* Reflexive pronoun sees around (4)
19.* See 3 down (5)
20.* A time of drinking, nearly like Horace—*tempus* _ _ _ _ _ _ _ (7)
21. Did a Roman *discipulus* sit behind this for writing part of an ode—skiving? (4)
23.* Tacitus claimed to write _ _ _ _ / _ _ _ / _ _ *studio* (4, 3, 2)

Clues Down

1. Principal hall of ancient Greek house—'ome with gran in a mess? (7)
2.*/22.*/19ac.* By force of (and) arms (2, 2, 5)
3.*/12ac.*/9ac.* "It's now or never" (3, 4, 3, 7)
4.*/5.*/2ac.* "You ain't nothing but a hound-dog" (= hunting dog) (2, 5, 2, 4, 5, 9)
6. Shaped like a (Latin) shield—round about statue, roughly? (7)
7.* (S)he arms (5)
14.* You (s.) will not go (not Egypt's sacred bird!) (3, 4)
15. A compound of Latin sodium carbonate in tried form (7)
16. Modern Greek dish of minced meat, aubergine, tomatoes, and cheese (7)
17*./13 ac.* "I don't have a wooden heart" (5, 3, 3, 7)
18.* *Nisi*, or a treacherous Greek (2, 3 or 5)

D8 vegetable spy

Clues Across

1.* Lo and behold, a Latin palindrome (4)
3. Latin "Look! A rich man!" yields a crop of chicory (7)
7.* Alas! (4)
8. A javelin in Latin and sun, going west, becomes the god of Rome's bakers (8)
9. The nightingale might mope—a hill where Tereus let slip her tongue! (9)
13. Father of Cronus (6)
14.* An augur's curved staff (6)
16.* Out of* ten you soundly *es* to make thin (9)
19. Catullus' poetic contradiction? I too made wild version (3, 2, 3)
20. See 5d (4)
21. Greek Furies in Ireland poetically? Indeed (7)
22.* Hey! He and us together? (4)

Clues Down

1.* E.g. example (8)
2. To do with a priest (Church Latin derivation) (8)
3.* You will extract, take out (6)
4. A Classical Noah? Did he get stoned with Pyrrha? (9)
5.*, 18.*, 20ac.* Julius Caesar's zealous comment! (4, 4, 4)
6. *Sic ita*—neither good nor bad (2-2)
10. Plenty Lou mixed up richly (9)
11. *varium et _ _ _ _ _ _ _ _ semper/femina* (Virgil, on Dido) (8)
12. Sad rites for minor planets? (8)
15.* We stand (6)
17.* Place (s.)! (4)
18. See 5 (4)

D9 X marks the spot—the great adventure

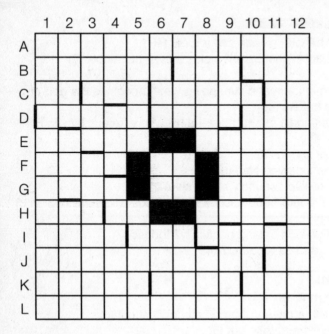

The purpose of this crossword is to reveal the names of a great ancient hero of myth and his followers who sailed east to…but that would be to give the game away. The leader will be found at A1—5; six of his friends will then follow him clockwise round the edge of the board from A6—B1.

Aha! But what were they looking for? This too will be revealed by marking an X-shape right through the centre of the completed crossword—one diagonal from D4 to I9, the other from D9 to I4.

What, however, is the four-letter square in the centre of the puzzle doing? This contains the vital advice "Destroy!", in Latin—four letters, in the order G7, G6, F6, F7. Fill that in, and you are already some way to discovering the object of the quest.

One other subtle feature. Adventurers never get there first

time—they go forward and back, up and down, in and out, and generally shake it all about. So will the answers to the clues—some running left to right, others right to left, some down, some up. *So follow the directions of the clues very carefully indeed.*

Cold towels and reviving mint juleps are strongly recommended.

Clues Across (Left—Right; Right—Left)

B1—6* Coil, whorl (acc.); **9—7*** Nothing; **12—10** Sea nymph

C1—2* And; **3—5*** Enough; **6—10*** Oxen/cows; **11—12*** It

D1—5* To be touched; **9—6*** I trust *this dog!*; **10—12*** Eggs

E1—5* On the shoulder; **8—12** *Ligulae*—tie up Alec's?

F1—4 On the pedestal low down; **12—9*** Three

G1—4 *Scindere, divellere*; **9—12*** Having arisen (m. pl.), alternative is back!

H1—3* Eat! Produce (s.)!; **4—5*** 99; **12—8*** With a fish

I1—4 *Casa Gallica* for holidays?; **5—7** *Gallina*; **12—8*** gaping, yawning (s.)

J1—10* Star-gazer/teller; **11—12** *Equus ferreus*, seen briefly here?

K5—1* Throw back! (s.); **6—9** Stem of Latin lion; **10—12*** Countryside

Clues Down (Up—Down; Down—Up)

2A—D* Suitable (f.) up at Pennsylvania; **G—E*** Her (acc.); **H—L*** Learn! (s.)

3E—A* Sword; **L—F*** Sending (s.) woolly gloves!

4A—C* Pray! I plough up; **F—D** Unit of work—loveless therefore*?; **L—G** Sea nymph

5A—E* Tribe, race, class; **H—L*** By a band of singers/dancers

6A—D* Both; **L—I*** He's that one

7A—D *Glaeba*, or 150 overdosed; **I—L** Saturnalia today—wild K6!

8E—A* Wife of Augustus; **H—I** You are (s.); **J—L** *pars Indiae*

9D—A *Paludes*; **H—E _ _ _ _** *nostra* if the Mafia; **I—L*** Now

10A—B *ad*; **C—G*** Father-in-law—crazy score!; **L—H*** She-bears (acc.)

11A—H* All together (m.); **L—I*** Of the East Wind

D10 Up, up and away

Clues Across

1*/5d.* Motto of the Royal. Flying Corps (3, 5, 2, 5)

9. Diana in Greek (7)

10. Top of the house of Athens! (5)

11.* You (s.) were going (4)

13. *Magni patres*, *avi*—or great commercials! (8)

14.* Run (s.)! Sounds like hot stuff! (5)

15.* As—but not the coin (2)

16. An animal without feet, like a slug in Greek (4)

19.* (Too) late (4)

20.* Wit—and pepper? (3)

21.*/23d.*/27d.*/8d.* Horace's nagging back-seat driver might call for Prozac! (4, 7, 5, 4, 4)

22. Greek god of war (4)

24.*/25d.* On the quiet—from a Roman historian (2, 6)

25.* For the bull (dat.) (5)

26. Strong—mouse* god of the house* with heart of copper (8)

28.* *Inter _ _ _ _* (amongst other things) (4)

30.* He/she plays (5)

31.* Outstanding (n.) in E. sign somehow (7)

32. Impromptu, on the spur of the moment—out of time, almost, Al (10)

Clues Down

2. *Ulmi* (4)

3. Convince us with 22 somehow (6)

4. *instructi*, like legions ready for battle (5, 2)

6.* Aeneas gave Mnestheus a breastplate for a prize, to be an "ornament and protection" (*Aeneid V.262*) (5, 2, 7)

7.* Catullus' osculatory demands (2, 2, 5, 5)

12.* *Ne _ _ _ _ _ ultra crepidam*—cobbler, stick to your last (5)

13. *Herba* (5)

16. *Ara* (5)

17.* Works musically! (5)

18. Glory words in Christian hymn to God reportedly medico's science (8)

29.* Possibly it's a clue to those things of yours (n. pl.) (4)

Course E: Cheese *(Difficillimum)*
E1 Fairground warning

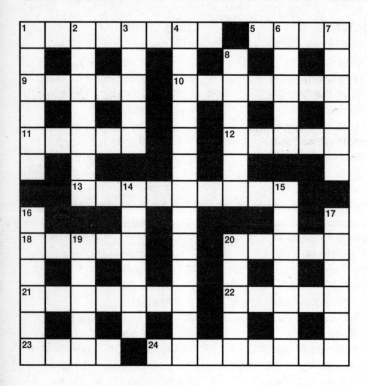

Clues Across

1. Muse of Epic poetry or summon Io for physical education? (8)
5.* A sign. See 18ac (4)
9. Weeping for her lost children, she was petrified (5)
10. Pertaining to Publius Naso, Roman poet (7)
11.* I call out (5)
12.* (S)he wears away, rubs out—sort of trite (5)
13.* "Ours it is…" See 14d (6, 3)
18.*/5.* Touch wood—superstitiously (5, 4)
20.* For a boy (*maxima debetur ..... reverentia* Juvenal xiv 47) (5)
21.* Roman army subaltern officer hidden in blockade—curious! (7)
22.* They were going (5)
23.* I know (4)
24. Greek hero, son of Tydeus—historian Cassius and an ancient Persian people? (8)

Clues Down

1.*, 16*. May you sing, may you praise (6, 6)
2. Priest of Apollo who attacked the Wooden Horse and got in a tight squeeze! (7)
3.* I shall have gone (5)
4.* *Dulce et decorum est* _ _ _ / _ _ _ _ _ _ / _ _ _ _ (Horace *Odes* ii 13) (3, 6, 4)
6.* Greater—almost like an English ex-Prime Minister! (5)
7. XC or LXXXX (6)
8.* Ribbons, sacrificial headband (6)
14.*, 13ac.* Quintilian's claim for Roman style of writing—very Juvenal! (6, 6, 3)
15. Statius' poem for The Seven—one in the worst style! (7)
16.* See 1down (6)
17. Constellation containing Arcturus—a Greek ox-driver (6)
19.* Footwear—so 201! (5)
20. Aged King of Troy is one in a baby buggy! (5)

E2 Word-square

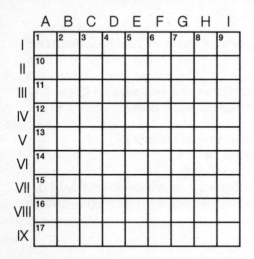

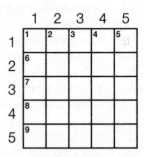

This puzzle features word-chains—that means that the last letter or letters of the answer to a clue are used to start the answer to the next clue. Where the last clue of the complete line has brackets round it, the whole line makes a Latin word—and the bracketed clue should be it!

Take, for example, the chain at I (overlapping letters underlined): *ego sum* = I am; unit of current = <u>amp</u>; group of *leones* = <u>p</u>ride; the same* = <u>idem</u>. This makes *iampridem*—and, lo beholdque, the last square-bracketed clue [=long ago*] shows we have got it right. Note that not all the lines have a final bracketed clue.

But there is yet more ingenuity to come. When the grid is complete, mark off the following lines (which together make up the central 'square' of the puzzle):

iiiCDEFG; ivCDEFG; vCDEFG; viCDEFG; viiCDEFG

Then transfer them in that order to the smaller grid, and you will find that you have the famous Cirencester Word-Square, which runs the same forwards, backwards, up and down.

Clues Across

I. *Ego sum*; unit of current; group of *leones*; the same* [= long ago*]

II. O spring*; truly*; and*; apex, point; ratio of circumference to diameter of a circle

III. Roman burning fiddler?*; wheels (acc. pl.)*; *status quo*, *ut est* (2, 2)

IV. Out of*; "outside of" as prefix; work* *cit.*; through*; you were (s.)*; to wit, namely* (abb.)

V. Tame, family animal; seek* (s.) !; hold* (s.)!; *rete*; teetotal; you* (acc. s.)

VI. Altar*; to plough*; I crawl*; where? (French); University of Alabama (abb.)

VII. Pig*; America; enough* (abb.); *ad*; pile of rocks, rocky height; *dextra/sinistra*; 950*

VIII. *Unus*; look*! A printing measure; female monk; and (German); wave*; gold

IX. Street (abb.); (s)he stands*; sol-fa note; triumphant cry*; numerals [= staging posts, guards*]

Clues Down

A. Cry of triumph*; charged particle; scorpion*; *ut* or small coin; *sic*; bone*; international 'help' code

B. Hail!*; out of*; one who annoys; *curre*!; small pig [= they have carried off *or* ridden away*]

C. French sea; with wine pure and undiluted*; decay; Territorial Army (abb.); Roman coin*; *mare*

D. On behalf of*; near*; through*; age; *formica*; they were* [=they hurry*]

E. In the matter of*; and*; you (acc.)*; net*; X; hold*; (s)he holds*; you*; of you*

F. *Id*; so*; (biblical) weed; extended play (record); Italian river; cry of disbelief (1, 2) [= I put back, replace*]

G. Gods*; Pluto or Hades*; enough*, or *sedit*; *ad*; alternatively; road (abb.); District Notary (abb.)

H. (Greek) prefix above, over, on; sixteenth letters of Greek alphabet; street (abb.); you* (s.); arm bone not new*; aged* (abb.) [= letters*]

I. Third sol-fa notes; *Senatus Consultum*** (abb.); Common Era; her* (acc.) or I may go*; I am backward mouse* [= let us mingle*]

E3 What is truth?

Clues Across

1.*/13d.*/2d.*/11.* Every man to his opinion (4, 7, 3, 10)
3.* Have! Hold! (4)
7.* See 5 (4)
8. In Greek, of the ear (4)
10.* For God (dat.) (3)
14.* Place for leisurely learning (6)
15. *Radix* (4)
16. *Calceus* (4)
17.* "In the same place" (abbrev.) (4)
18. The vale of Tempe in Thessaly was the equivalent of *this* paradise for Greeks and Romans (4)
19.* I have recaptured, taken back (6)
20.* Caesar, "you are that body" on the thirteenth! (2, 2, 6)
23. *Fecit*; loveless Carthaginian Queen (3)
24. Her swan song after Zeus' visit? (4)
26.* By skill, technique (4)
27.* Hers (acc. f. s.) (4)
28.* Let it stand (4)

Clues Down

1.* Pilate's question in Latin—anagram of 6 (4, 3, 7)
2.* See 1ac (3)
3.* "This was in (my) prayers" (Horace, *Satires* II.vi.1) (3, 4, 2, 5)
4.* "Hercules from his foot"—all you need, to recognise a great man (2, 4, 8)
5.* Caesar: *Veni,* 7 across, _ _ _ _ (4)
6.* "It is the man who is present"—anagram of 1 down (3, 3, 3, 5)
8. *Oratio obliqua* (2)
9.* *Est* (2)
12. Author of the quote at 1 across (7)
13.* See 1 across
21.* Let it be (4)
22.* Reflexive pronoun (2)
23.* Give! (2)
25. Another name for Pluto or Hades (3)

E4 Screen *stellae*

The aim of this cinematic crossword is to identify famous sayings of famous stars. These appear in Latin (naturally) in the shaded squares. The *stellae*, some with names partly in Latin, are listed below, and their famous sayings are to be filled in alongside them when the crossword is complete.

Clark Fastigium
_ _ / _ _ _ _, / _ _ _ _ / _ _ _, / _ _ _ _ _ _ _ / _ _ _ / _ _ _ _ _
(12 [first two letters] / 33 / 27d / 6d / 22 / 19 / 46 + 17)
James Cagney
_ _ / _ _ _ _ _ _ ! / _ _ / _ _ _ _ _ _ / _ _ _ _ _ _ ! (13 / 2 / 13 / 2 / 31)
Clint Silvaorientalis
_ _ _ ! / _ _ _ / _ _ / _ _ _ _ _ _ _ ! (14 / 46ac / 49 / 15)

Said to 'Ossa' McCoy (*Migratio ad Sidera*)

_ _ / _ _ _ _ _ _ _ _ _ _ / _ _ _ _ _ _ / _ _ _ _ _ _ _ _ !

(6d [1st two letters] / 42 + 6ac / 34 / 27ac)

Mae Occidens

_ _ _ _ _ _ _ _ / _ _ _ _ _ _ _ / _ _ / _ _ / _ _ _ _ _

(29 + 50 / 10 / 49 / 6d [1st two letters] / 48)

de Christophoro Reeve

"_ _ _ _ _ / _ _ _ _ ? / _ _ _ _ _ / _ _ _ _ _ _ _ _ ? / _ _ _ /

_ _ _ _ _ _ _ _ / _ _ _ " (9 + 44 [1st two letters] / 32? / 9 + 44 [1st two letters] / 4 + 20d? / 19 / 40 + 39 / 9)

As usual, these words are not clued, and there are some "unchecked" letters.

Clues Across

1. Alternative for gold in Oregon (2)
3.* "_ _ _ *victis!*" Alas! (3)
12.* Thing (3)
16. Wild riots in threes (5)
20.* I bare all (4)
21.* Scattered, spread out (acc. pl. m.) (7)
26. Hebrew name for healer in a Roman coin (3)
28.* With heat (abl. s.) (6)
35. Sweat it out here with plenty of 28ac (5)
36. *Venit* (past time) (4)
38. Recto (abbrev.) (2)
45. Broken nib might go here? (3)
47.* Well done! Bravo! (2)

Clues Down

3.* 95 (2)
5.* See printer's measure (2)
7. Italian for three (3)
8.* _ _ *laudamus,* _ _ *benedicimus* (2)
11.* Deaf (f. s.) (5)
17.* A cry of triumph (2)
18. *Phoca* or *signum* (4)
23.* Bring! (s.) iron (3)
24. *ita, sic*—bone* turned up (2)
25.* If (2)
28.* Hundreds apiece (n. pl.) (7)
30. Sodium (abbrev.) in North America (2)
37.* He/she curtails a rat-t that's moving around (5)
41.* Where or when (3)
43. Roman Catholic (abbrev.) (2)
44.* Short for *neu* (3)
46. _ _ Manchu (2)

E5 Roscius' boar

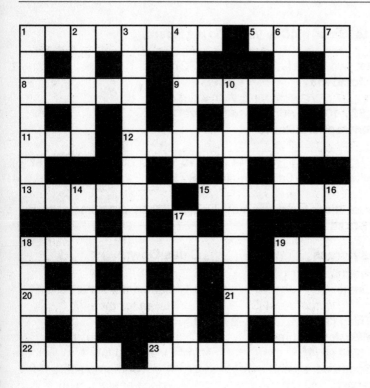

Clues Across

1. Term for an actor, derived from the inventor of Greek tragedy (8)
5.* Boar (4)
8.* I am thin, lean in horrible cameo (5)
9. Richly fertile—based on Latin for "udder" (7)
11. Minerva's symbol (3)
12.* He/she aggravates a sore (9)
13. Virgil's great epic (6)
15. *Delevit* and 'e shaved, reportedly (6)
18. Pearl in Greek, a cross between a girl's name and a spread (9)
19.* _ _ _ *vobiscum* (3)
20. *Iterum gusta!*—stir tea and rest up (7)
21.* Old man (acc.) (5)
22. Winter capital of Persia in matchless USA (4)
23.* We are able (8)

Clues Down

1.*/18.* O _ _ _ _ _ _ _, o _ _ _ _ _ —not just on newspaper fashions! (7, 5)
2. Sounds like forty in Roman numerals—be superior (5)
3. First to land and die at Troy—is pale and routs frantically (11)
4.* *Omnes _ _ / _ _ _ _*: all to a man (2, 4)
6. Wife of Cephalus, hunting victim or crisp fatality? (7)
7.* Smiled, laughed, sir, it's comical (5)
10.* See 19
14. Mountain on Ithaca stonier likely to collapse (7)
16.* We have said (7)
17. Author of 1, 18 down
18.* See 1 down
19.*/10.* What the masses want—according to Juvenal (5, 2, 9)

E6 In Wonderland

ac.. the title of this crossword, review your Lewis Carroll and off you go. First of all, some questions to set you up.

Who* 1ac. (3) is she? She is 3ac. (5), in English. Where is she? She is in 15* 50d.* (5, 9). Wonderful!

Now you can mix and match. Here followeth the story of OOPS nearly gave away her name; but if you prefer, you can go straight to the clues beneath the story to give yourself a head start. Real gluttons, once they have completed the crossword, can go a step further—possibly too far—as you will see at the end of the clues.

After the 2d.* waves (5) of the 25d.* (7) of 67ac.* (10), she met the 14d.* white (5) 45 ac.* (9). On a 80* mushroom (7) sat a 69* (5) with a 62* small tube (6) 20* of *tabac.us* (gen.) (6). In the *culina* of the 37d.* duchess (7), a 22d.* (6) turned into a 42* (3). She saw in an *arbore* the 8ac.* Cheshire (9) 32* (5) 40ac.* with a smile (4) who left only a 68d.* (6). Around the *mensa* were gathered the 53* March (7) 4d.* (5), the 56d.* (6) 29ac.* (of) hat (6) 55ac.* seller (8), and the 28d.* (4), a sort of 87ac. (3). The 64* was playing a *lusus* that needed a 29d.* flamingo (12) and a 90ac.* (7). On the edge 35d.* of the shore (4) was a 36ac. (4), but it ended in court with the 31* king (3), 64* (6), 21* Knave (4) of 45* (7).

Clues Across *(clues down on p. 96)*

16. A shout; *hoc anno* (abbrev.) (2)
17. Old Greek coin—one-sixth of a drachma (4)
18.* It (2)
19. *Pater* briefly in Pennsylvania (2)
23.* Died; on account of (2)
24.* Crafty; sly (7)
27. Final word in prayer for *nostri*, we hear (4)
28. *Dorcas africanus* (3)
34. *Fraus* of 16 and a wild ox (4)
38. *Magnus, maior _ _ _ _* but mouse* is missing; long coat (4)XXX
39.* Bacchic revels (5)
41. Trick; *captivus*; short for *contra* (3)

44. Bring forth an Eastern represented (3)
46. Nerve cell—neither* nor sent back (6)
48. Letter of Greek alphabet that's holy (2)
49. Old city expressing note of hesitancy (2)
50. *Ancilla* (4)
57.* About (abbrev.) (2)
59.* Bears I have urged on (4)
60.* She was love Muse (5)
63.* You (s.) overwhelm (6)
70.* Two (2)
71.* I drink up (5)
72.* Roman wear (acc. s.) (5)
74.* Approach! (s.) with foreign aid (3)
77.* Effort striving—is sun eclipsed? (5)

E6 In Wonderland *(continued)*

78.* Having given birth (f. s.) despite a poor diet (5)
83. Short girl's name 50/49* (3)
85. *Desertor* from English gardener's not right (8)
88. *Simulac.rum* in Greek church (4)
91.* Too late (4)

Clues Down

3.* But or *ad* (2)
5.* Angry (m. pl.) (5)
6. Crown creditor (abbrev.) (2)
7. *Edit* teas spread out (4)
8. 101* A—an agency for *speculatores* (3)
9. *Pudor* (5)
10.* Be quiet (s.)! (4)
11.* Joyful cry (2)
12.* By, from (2)
13. *Nemo* (5)
26. Thank 11* for cab (4)
30.* Manner; custom (3)
33.* Out of (2)
36. 500 in loud noise (3)
38. *Lugere* for short time over urn (5)
40. The smallest *porcus* (4)

41. This is one *indicium* or *vestigium* (4)
43. For one round pearl (4)
47. *Deus Aegyptius solis* (2)
48. *Fluere leniter* up, right and left around (4)
51.* *Idem ac.* 3 (2)
52.* Rac.ecourse at Sparta (6)
54.* Laws; rights (4)
55.* I have conquered (4)
58.* *Idem ac.* 12 (2)
61.* By altars (abl. pl.) (4)
65. Acid salt you soundly value (5)
66.* *Senatus Consultum* (abbrev.) (2)
73. Written by Horac.e (3)
74.* Hide (s.)! A bid that's strange (4)
75. *Cerva* (3)
76.* 49 (2)
79. *Aetas* (3)
81. *Avis australis quae non volat* (3)
82. *Nos* (2)
84. *Glac.ies* (3)
86. *Anno regni* (abbrev.) (2)
89. Negative (2)

Gluttons for punishment only

When you have completed the crossword, transfer the cell numbers from the main grid to the following puzzle:

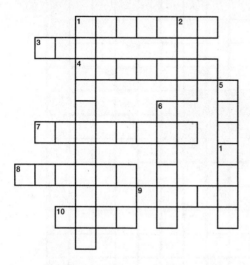

1ac.: j10 / o8 / e15 / c1 / j15 / k2 / o13
1d.: j10 / e11 / h13 / m1 / e2 / q16 / j6 / l6 / l8 / e6 / k17
2: d10 / p5 / a17 / g8
3: a1/ g16 / i2
4: l6 / g7 / i14 / d5 / o9 / n7 / d3
5: a1 / l4 / m10 / i17 / j12 / m7 / f12
6: p10 / n16 / d13 / f7/ d7/ d11
7: e13 / k13 / m4 / p15 / j8 / b17 / p11 / l17
8: p7 / i3 / l2 / j1 / a12 / q17
9: k9 / g9 / c5 / k14 / h2
10: l13 / q9 / g11 / q3

Then put the Latin words in the following order, for a merry little poem by the same author, mocking "Twinkle, twinkle". Ooh! Sacrilege!
10ac.; 1d.; 5; 2; 8; 9; 6; 1ac.; 7+ 3; 4

E7 In your hat

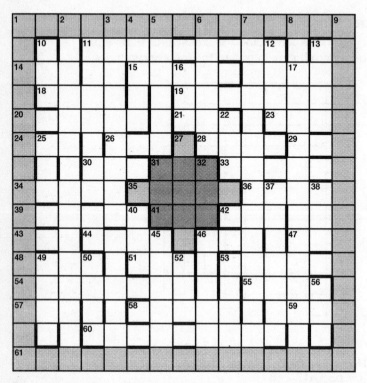

Beginning at 1ac. and running clockwise round the perimeter of this crossword and ending up at 14 are four lines of Latin, every schoolboy's favorite Latin poem (you have been warned):

Line 1: 6, 5, 3, 5; line 2: 6, 6; line 3: 6, 3, 2, 7;line 4: 6, 6.

For the final word of the fourth line, go to the centre of the crossword and insert "i" at 27, "n" between 33 and 42, "i" between 45 and 46, and "s" at 35. That leaves two letters to complete the poem! What must they be? You can use the shaded area in the middle of the puzzle to illustrate it. The words you need are not clued, and there are unchecked letters. Taken together, these letters make up "Circumstance—a famous road".

Clues Across

11.* Highly decorated (acc. pl. f.) (9)
15. Sounds like stormy weather for the Celts (5)
17.* Through (3)
18.* For the citadel (dat. s.) (4)
19.* He/she will have fortified (fut. perf.) (8)
20.* Being silent (pres. part.) (6)
21.* May you go (2 s. of pres. subj.) or those (acc. pl. f.) (3)
23.* Advise! (s.) (4)
24.* Where (3)
26.* Law, right, justice (3)
28.* Stay! (s.) (4)
29. A *taberna* (3)
30.* He/she is (3)
33.* Wider, broader (6)
34. *Belua* (5)
36.* With feeling (abl.s.) (5)
39.* Goaty Greek woodland gods with tails and long ears (6)
42.* Power, help (3)
43.* To use (3)
44. _ _ _ _ and Abel (4)
46.* Lion (3)
47.* By use (abl. s.) (3)
48.* On a pedestal (abl. s)—low spot in Yankee stadium? (4)
51. Dick Gumshoe? (3)
53.* Wandering (pres. part.) (6)
54.* I set up, establish (8)
55.* For you (4)
57.* O river nymph (voc.) (3)
58.* Pile up! (s.) (5)
59. Indian black bean seed found in sour dough (3)
60.* Uneven (n.) (9)

Clues Down

2.* Very well drilled (m. pl.) (15)
3.* For the management of (provincial) government (dat. s.) (15)
4.* You ask (2 s.) (5)
5.* Having been ploughed (m. s. of perf. part.) (6)
6.* Safe, alive, well (acc. s. f.) (6)
7.* Martial's "stingy dole hand-out" (7, 8)
8.* They will draw near, get close (15)
10. E.g. *Aquae Sulis*, famous for its waters (3)
11.* You (s.) will come to, agree with (7)
12.* Pig (acc. s.) (4)
13.* Then, next (4)
16.* Buy (s.)! (3)
22.* Salt, wit (3)
25. *Apis* (3)
37.* To be hungry (7)
38.* Another pig or arrest for suspicious behavior! (3)
40.* He/she has gone (3)
45.* Neither m. nor f. (6)
46.* An augur's staff or trumpet (6)
49.* A duck (4)
50.* Even if; and yet (4)
52.* My! Heart (3)
53.* At the birthplace of Parmenides (locative) (5)
56.* Anger (3)

E8 Triplets

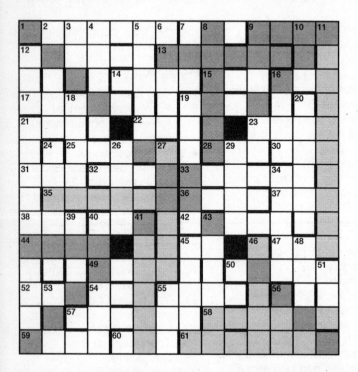

Four famous trios have each lost one of their members. Can you find them ? 'X' will mark the spot—with a little bit of help from HIYA!

As usual, the names that you are looking for are unclued and have to be reconstructed from the answers to the remaining clues. Watch out for unchecked letters.

Group 8d: members 11, 58 and ?
Group 9ac: members 27, 61 and ?
Group 13ac: members 5, 35 and ?
Group 44ac: members 41, 46 and ?

Remember: HIYA!

Clues Across

1. Boat with three banks of oars (7)
7.* I (3)
12. Use the car to discover an ancient country (6)
14. Paradise, like the Elysian Fields (4)
15. *Aither*, the upper _ _ _ (3)
16.* Latin on tombstones (3)
17.* For an old woman lain ill I find (5)
19. *Dolorosus* on sinking yacht —time out (4)
21. *Auxilium* (3)
22.* Reflexive pronoun (2)
23.* Smell (4)
25. Jewish founding father— his name means *risus* (5)
28. *Ecce* you, we hear, makes a name (3)
30.* I buy (3)
31.* For a respectful (man) (3)
32. *Malus, malignus* (4)
33. If cold manipulate a pearl round your *auris* (6)
36. *Aristae* (of barley, etc.) (4)
37. A mystic line *per agros* (3)
38. Greek *e* (3)
40. *Balaena interfector* or hundred* (3)
42.* Let him/her know (5)
45.* A short laugh *hoc anno* (abbrev.) (2)
47. *Simia* or *imitari* (3)
49. Marco *Mercator* (4)
50.* I have deserved (5)
52. Ancient negative—7d. up (3)
54. *Glacies* (3)
55. *Liber* but not read (4)
57. *Ego non facio* (1, 2, 3)
59.* To be thrown out (4)
60.* Night (3)

Clues Down

2.* German river (gen. s.) (5)
3.* Anger (3)
4. *Longurii* or *maledicit* (5)
6.* To be in want (5)
7. *Aetas longa* (3)
9. *Tibi* or *vobis* (3, 3)
10.* Of you (s.) (3)
12.* Yours (s. f.) (3)
16. *Equitare* (4)
18. *Stultus* (5)
19. He left Dido, but still a hero for Virgil (6)
20. A general rival of Caesar (6)
21.* Grasp (s.)! (10)
24.* Chests—not the pulmonary sort (6)
26. *Adfirmare, adseverare* (4)
29.* Ash trees (4)
34. *Ara* (5)
39.* With skill (4)
40.* Town (gen. s.) (6)
43.* _ _ _ _ _ *emptor*, let the buyer beware (6)
45.* Hairy (n. pl.) (5)
48.* Dagger (5)
51.* Thus, so (3)
53.* Leisure time (gen. s.) (3)
55. *Vulpes* (3)
56. *Sucus*, or *subruere* (3)

E9 Christmas I: From oxen to pears

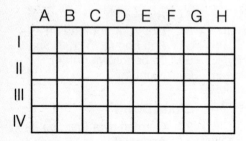

This is a two-part puzzle. First, tackle the little crossword above. It prepares you for the bigger puzzle that follows.

Columns (down)
A. Give* 51 for this surrealist painter
B.* As 999
C. An _ _ _ _ house stores hops or wild oats
D. Translate and reverse *ego et*
E. Errors excepted (abbrev.) / 1,500*
F. Central Intelligence Agency (abbrev.) / east (abbrev.)
G. It* / touch-down
H. Chinese Chairman / *rex* (abbrev.)

When the grid is full, read it *boustrophedon*, i.e. Ai—Hi / Hii—Aii / Aiii—Hiii / Hiv—Aiv (*boustrophedon*, ox-turning, like an ox going up a field and turning round to come back). You will be able to read six Latin words introducing this crossword. These will help you with the shaded answers, which are required to complete the song.

As usual, these answers are not clued. They have also been slightly adapted so that, the puzzle brilliantly finished, you can all stand round the blazing log-fire and sing along.

The completed song makes up a list of objects. In the clues we tell you how many of each object there are.

Clues Across *(clues down on p. 104)*

(clues down on p. 104)

1.* **ELEVEN OF THESE**
8.* **HELPING THE SINGLETON ON THE LIST**
10.* It (2)
11.* The Muse of astronomy (6)
13.* **FOUR OF THESE**
15.* **EIGHT DO THIS**
16. Paying guest (abbrev.) (2)
18. *Aquae Sulis*, where Romans took the waters (3)
19.* You are (s.) (2)
20.* By, from (2)
21.* **NEEDED FOR THE EIGHT**

E9 Christmas I: From oxen to pears (*cont.*)

23. Thalium (abbrev.) (2)
25.* Thing (acc. s.) (3)
26.* 551 (3)
27.* As; in order to (2)
28.* **FIVE OF THESE**
31.* **TWELVE DO THIS**
33.* *Dulce et decorum est pro patria _ _ _ _* (4)
34. New Greek; one in need of repairing (3)
35. Alto; alternate; altitude (abbrev.) (3)
37.* **SEVEN OF THESE**
38.* With excess, debauchery (abl. s.) (4)
40.* Dice (5)
42.* **ONE OF THESE**
44.* _ _ _ *Gestae*, Augustus' achievements (3)
45.* Go (pl.)! (3)
46.* Coin (2)
48.* _ _ _ *ardua ad astra* (3)
49.* **NINE OF THESE**
54.* Mouth bone (2)
55.* Gods, or 501 (2)
56.* Water, lottery, voting jars (acc. pl.) (5)

Clues Down

1.* Be afraid of *tempus*! (4)
2.* 13/15th of month (4)
3.* Yokes/ridges (4)
4.* Frequently (6)
5.* **WHAT THE SEVEN ARE DOING**
6. Hospital Department for *aures, naso, guttur* (abbrev.) (3)
7.* If (2)
8.* Four (2)
9. God of the Seas (7)
12.* At the house of, or one eaten at Christmas (4)
14.* **TEN OF THESE**
17.* **THREE OF THESE**

22.* For them (dat. pl.) (3)
24.* **TWO OF THESE**
28.* Love (s.)! (3)
29.* He/she might refuse; tell on if aroused (6)
30.* 51 (2)
31. *Stipendium* is _ _ _ for soldiers (3)
32.* **SIX OF THESE**
36.* **THE TWELVE NEED THIS**
37.* With a boxing glove (abl. s.) (6)
39.* 499 (2)
41.* Weather, air, mist (3)
42.* **WHERE THE ONE IS**
43. *Feles* (3)
47.* But if one of seven deadly ones (3)
48.* Foot (3)
50.* To, at (2)
51.* 51 (2)
52. Right Reverend (abbrev.) (2)
53.* About (abbrev.) (2)

E10 Christmas II: Rufus

In this puzzle we will teach you the first and third verses of another well-known Christmas song. To do this, we must introduce you to Caesar's Amazing Secret Code—though not quite amazing enough, for obvious reasons.

Caesar used a special cipher to send messages to his friends. Each letter in any message was replaced by a cipher letter which was *three places further on in the alphabet*. Thus, where Caesar would normally have written A, he wrote instead D, and the whole system was known as Caesar's D Alphabet.

The song words of **Grid A** will be solved by using this D Alphabet. You will find the song words among the clues, and the word number that accompanies them tells you where in the song they come. When you have solved **Grid A** and put the words in the right order, you will have the first verse of the song. Await instructions for **Grid B**.

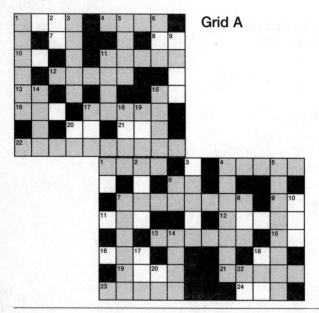

Grid A

Grid B

GRID A *(Grid B clues are on p. 108)*
Clues Across
1. Computer *stultus* (4)
4.* **SONG WORD SEVEN = VWDW**
7.* Two, or I have gone (2)
8. Cry of surprise* this year (abbrev.) (2)
10.* **SONG WORD NINE = VL**
11.* **SONG WORD SIX = UXEHU**
12.* **SONG WORDS FOUR AND TWELVE = QDVXV**
13. Musical note sounds like a drink (2)
15.* Six by force (2)
16.* I buy (3)
17.* **SONG WORD THREE = FHUYH**
20.* Shout of joy or *decem* (2)
21.* Weather or air (3)
22.* **SONG WORD FOURTEEN = FRQIODJUDW**

Clues Down
1.* **SONG WORD TWO = QDVXWH**
2. Religious Instruction (abbrev.) (2)
3.* **SONG WORD ELEVEN = GLFDP**
5.* **SONG WORDS FIVE AND THIRTEEN = WXXV**
6. Definite article lacking in Latin (3)
9.* Field, land (gen. s.) (4)
11.* **SONG WORD ONE = UXIH**
14.* **SONG WORD EIGHT = LPPR**
15.* **SONG WORD TEN = YHUD**
17. A mountain pass, Colonel, shortly (3)
18. *Panniculus* (3)
19.* Spring (3)
20. See 10 (2)

E10 Christmas II: Rufus *(continued)*

The principle of the D Alphabet is extendable across the whole alphabet. You could construct an E Alphabet, or an M Alphabet, or... Grid B exploits these possibilities, as you will see.

GRID B
Clues Across
1.*/6.* SONG WORD SEVEN = [B alphabet] *WVMUV*
4.* SONG WORD THREE = [C alphabet] *XGPKV*
7.* **SONG WORD ONE = [G alphabet] *TKHARUYU***
11.* For the gods or god of the Underworld (3)
12.* Showy display; procession (5)
13.* **SONG WORD TEN = [M alphabet] *FDMTQE***
15.* 999 (2)
16.* Let it be or sounds like *sede*! (3)
18.* But or *ad* (2)
19. *Surdus* (4)
21.* **SONG WORD NINE = [Q alphabet] *YELUC***
23.* **SONG WORD EIGHT = [T alphabet] *GHGGX***
24.* Through (3)

Clues Down
1.* Opposite of *recto* (abbrev.) (2)
2. *Hic iacet* = "Here _ _ _ _" (4)
3.* Blame (5)
4.* **SONG WORD TWO = [C alphabet] *XGURGTK***
5.* **SONG WORD FOUR = [F alphabet] *NZUUNYJW***
6.* **SONG WORD ELEVEN = [I alphabet] *BC***
7.* **SONG WORD SIX = [L alphabet] *YTETOZ***
8. Shouts of pleased surprise seep out, we hear (3)
10.* _ _ _ *pridem* (long ago) (3)
14.* **SONG WORD FIVE = [N alphabet] *EHSR***
17. *Decem* (3)
18.* Hail! (3)
20.* Abbreviation for *anno* or *ante* (2)
22.* Abbreviation for *opus* (2)

Solutions

A1 For starters

Notes

1/9 across. *Cave canem*, or "Beware of the dog", has been found in mosaic in the *vestibulum* or entrance hall to Roman houses, suitably illustrated too.

3. *Roma* is an anagram of *amor*, "love".

12. *Aurem* is the accusative of *auris*, "ear".

13. Stoics were a school of stern philosophers who taught in the *stoa poikile* ("painted porch") in Athens from the third century BC.

15. The Romans calculated their dates in relation to three fixed days each month: Kalends = 1st; Nones = 7th–9th; Ides = 13th–15th.

1 down. "Cato", a famous Stoic, is an anagram of "coat" (pointed by "ragged", i.e. confused, mixed-up).

9. Circe in Homer's *Odyssey* was the goddess who turned men into (male chauvinist?) pigs—but not Odysseus.

10. *Veni, vidi, vici* or "I came, I saw, I conquered" were Julius Caesar's famous words after defeating Pharnaces, son of Mithridates, at Zela in Pontus (Turkey) in 47 BC.

11. Acis, (who sounds like 'a sis[ter]), was a Sicilian shepherd, loved by Galatea. He was killed by his rival, the giant Polyphemus.

A2 The missing number

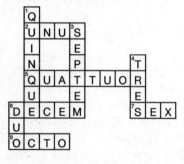

The missing number is *novem*.

Notes

Numbers offer splendid evidence for the family resemblance of those languages that all ultimately derive from what we call Indo-European, a long-lost language. Consider, for example, Latin *tres* (and French *trois*, Spanish *tres*, Italian *tre*, all derived direct from Latin), German *drei* (and

English *three*, from Anglo-Saxon *thri*, and Gothic *threis*—all these are Germanic languages), Celtic *tri*, Sanskrit *trayas*, Slavonic *trije*, Russian *tri*, Lithuanian *trys*, Hittite *tri*, and so on. In order to generate all these, we can work out that the Indo-European form must have been **treies*. The origins of the signs of the Roman numerical system—I, V, X and so on—are obscure. Sorry.

A3 Dem *ossa*, dem *ossa*

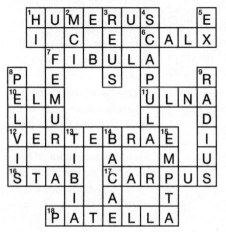

Key to the puzzle

A. tibia B. fibula C. pelvis D. patella E. vertebrae F. carpus G. humerus H. scapula I. femur J. calx K. ulna L. radius.

The pelvis is named from its basin-like shape; patella is a small plate; fibula is the brooch bone; the radius is the bone that rotates.

Notes

3 across. An anagram of "sure".

14. "We hear", because *bacae* sounds like Bacchae, or Maenads, female worshippers of Dionysus.

Medical terminology tends to be in Latin (and Greek) because Latin was the language of education up till the seventeenth century, and doctors learned their medical methods and terminology from ancient Greek and Roman doctors like Hippocrates, Galen and Celsus. Tough on the patients, but there it is. Even so, it was not until the ninenteenth century that germ-theory was confirmed—by Louis Pasteur, surely one of mankind's greatest benefactors. We should count our blessings. Anyway, the terminological convention having been established—even more powerfully in botany and entomology—the Graeco-Latin vocabulary is still ransacked when a new scientific term is required. Evidently a million insects still await proper naming, so Mr Wm. Gates's wonderfully exciting new *Encarta* dictionary is already useless.

A4 Proverbs I

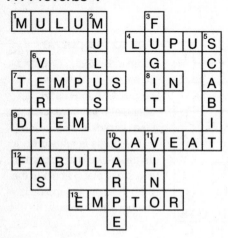

Proverbs

Caveat emptor "Let the buyer beware"
Tempus fugit "Time flies"
In vino veritas "In wine, truth"
Carpe diem "Seize the day"
Lupus in fabula "Talk of the devil" (lit. "The wolf in the story")
Mulus mulum scabit "The blind leading the blind" (lit. "The mule scratches the mule")

Notes

Latin was the language of education and international communication—especially in medicine, the law and the Church—till the seventeenth century. Consequently, where Latin offered a snappy way of expressing an idea, it tended to come into the everyday English usage of the educated élite. That is why there are so many Latin abbreviations, tags, mottoes and sayings in English, all the way from etc. and e.g. to the list above (see also, for example, the state mottoes of A8, B4 and B8 and the abbreviations of A10).

Excellently useful reference books in this field are James Morwood, *A Dictionary of Latin Words and Phrases* (Oxford 1998), and Jon Stone, *Latin for the Illiterati* (Routledge 1996).

A5 Your number's up

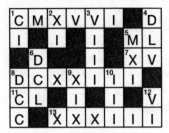

The words are CIVIC, CIVIL, DIM, LID, LIVID, MID, MILD, MIX, and VIM.

A6 Zodiac filler

Notes

20 across *Sepia* is Latin both for "cuttlefish" (from the Greek) and for the ink it extrudes, from which rich brown color pigments were prepared for water-based paints etc.

The Roman poet Manilius, writing about AD 10, lists the constellations of the zodiac in the following order: Aries, Taurus, Gemini, Cancer, Leo, Virgo, Libra, Scorpio, Sagittarius, Capricorn, Aquarius and Pisces, i.e. moving round the zodiac in a counter-clockwise, east-west direction. The Romans got these names by translating the Greek names, and of the Greek names, Taurus, Gemini, Cancer, Leo, Libra, Scorpio, Sagittarius, Capricorn and Pisces all derive from Babylonian terminology (c. 1000 BC). Babylonians had been observing and recording the heavens for *calendar* purposes for thousands of years; but it was Greeks of the fourth century BC who invented horoscopic astrology.

A7 The mink magpie

	A	B	C	D	E	F	G
I	D	O	M	I	N	U	S
II		A	D	I	V	E	S
III		T	N	D	I	S	E
IV		U	E		C	P	R
V		A	M	S	U	A	V
VI		N	R	E	P	U	U
VII		S	E	L	I	M	S

The list is the Latin version of "Tinker, Tailor...", and reads: *dominus—servus—miles—nauta—dives—pauper—mendicus—*(wait for it...)—*FUR.* Mink is a sort of fur (groan), and the magpie is, of course, a famously thieving bird.

A8 State mottoes I

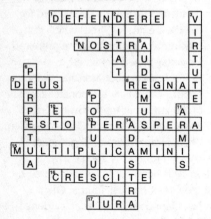

Alabama: *Audemus iura nostra defendere* "We dare to defend our rights"
Arizona: *Ditat Deus* "God enriches"
Arkansas: *Regnat populus* "The people rule"
Idaho: *Esto perpetua* "May she live for ever"
Kansas: *Ad astra per aspera* "To the stars through difficulties"
Maryland: *Crescite et multiplicamini* "Increase and multiply"
Mississippi: *Virtute at armis* "By valor and arms"

A9 Phrases and quotations

Notes

10/4 across Lit. "God from the machine". In the Greek theatre various mechanical devices could be used to make deities appear. The phrase now signifies an artificial, imposed solution to a difficulty, literary or otherwise.

11. Note the anagram "put airs".

1 down. *Et tu, Brute* ("You too, Brutus") are supposedly Caesar's dying words, but in fact he said them in Greek (*kai su, teknon*, "You too, my child/son"), and they probably mean "The same to you!", as Brutus stabbed him.

2. Romans believed the spirits of dead were either *lares familiares*—good—or *lemures/larvae*—bad—who roamed about haunting houses. Acrid beans were burned and kettles banged at the festival of *Lemuria* in May to get rid of them.

3. Lit. "state in which".

6. Confused critic 'e—i.e. an anagram of critic 'e. According to Pliny the Elder, the sight of the yellow golden oriole (Greek *ikteros*) helped to cure jaundice. But the bird always died as a result!

9/5. Catullus' love for Lesbia inspired the famous sentiment.

A10 Abbreviations

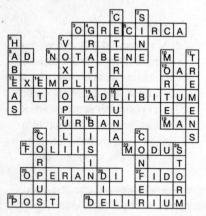

d.t.	*delirium tremens*	trembling madness
p.m.	*post mortem*	after death
m.o.	*modus operandi*	method of working
ad lib.	*ad libitum*	at pleasure; to one's liking
b.i.d.	*bis in die*	twice in the day
e.g.	*exempli gratia*	for the sake of an example
cf.	*confer*	compare; bring together
c.	*circa*	around; about
hab. cor.	*habeas corpus*	may you have the body
n.b.	*nota bene*	note well
s.d.	*sine die*	without a day (indefinitely)
vox. pop.	*vox populi*	the voice of the people
ff.	*foliis*	(following) pages; by leaves
etc.	*et cetera*	and other things; and the rest

See puzzle A4 for a brief discussion of such sayings.

B1 All-in Latin

Notes

19 across. "About" indicates an anagram of "roam".

6, 17. "Heavenly" because Castor and Pollux (Greek Polydeuces) were said to be the sons of Zeus by Leda. They were known together as the Dioscuri (Greek *Dios kouroi*, "young men of Zeus").

B2 Prof's palindrome

Notes

11 across. Hence "alibi"—you were in another place at the time.

15. *Atê* = ate, "took food".

4 down. "bottomless goddess", i.e. *dea* without the last letter, *de*.

B3 Furry white stickers

2 Letters: *tu; ab; si; CI*
3 Letters: *via; cum; qui; res; sed; rus; per; MCC*
4 Letters: *unda; toga; mare*
5 Letters: *mille; locus; murum*
6 Letters: *ferrum; cancer; turtur*
7 Letters: *milites*

The Poem: "Three Blind Mice"

Tres mures, tres mures!
Ecce currunt, ecce currunt!
Sequuntur agricolae feminam,
Caudas ea desecuit cultro,
Mirabile spectaculum visu—
Trium murium!

B4 State mottoes II

Maine: *Dirigo* "I direct"
Michigan: *Si quaeris paeninsulam amoenam, circumspice* "If you are looking for a lovely peninsula, look about you"
New Mexico: *Crescit eundo* "It grows by going" (Virgil)
North Carolina: *Esse quam videri* "To be rather than to seem"

Notes

10 across. "Place, we hear, for an eagle to nest": an eagle nests in an eyrie, which sounds like "eerie".

15. Catullus wrote a poem (no. 84) about Arrius, who hadded haitch to heverything.

36. "Wild" indicates anagram of "irate".

3 down. "Roughly" indicates anagram of "cored".

6. "Partly troubled by" indicates that the word is to be found in part of "queasiness".

7. "Losing right"—remove r from "Irma".

B5 Gods and goddesses

Notes

1 across. Jove or Jupiter or Zeus (Greek), king of the gods.

8. Every place had its *genius loci*—a presiding spirit.

11. Cupid, the Latin god of love (Greek Eros), is usually portrayed as a naked, winged infant armed with bow and arrows. Random, unthinking, you see. Shoots anywhere. So true.

12. Persephone, daughter of (21) Ceres (Greek Demeter), was taken to the underworld by Pluto. There she ate some pomegranate seeds, condemning her to spend six months underground (winter) but six months in the upper world (summer/harvest).

13. "Re-scene—review" i.e. an anagram of re-scene, meaning "criticise".

14. "So e's up": "up" = anagram, of "So 'e".

16. Orcus—also Dis, Hades, etc.

20. Bona Dea, "Good Goddess", was the name for various goddesses including Greek Cybele and Roman Fauna, who covered up male statues!

21. Ceres was goddess of crops (cf. cereal).

23. There were nine Muses—Clio, Euterpe, Thalia, Melpomene,

Terpsichore, Erato, Polyhymnia, Calliope, Urania. Learn them. They will almost certainly appear in many other crosswords. They do in this one.

1 down. Janus, god of the doorway, looked both ways. Hence he is the doorway to year.

2. Vesta was goddess of the hearth (Greek Hestia). In her temple in Rome, Vestal Virgins ensured her fire always burned.

6. Ariadne, daughter of King Minos of Crete, helped Theseus through the Minotaur's maze, only to be abandoned by him on the island of Naxos when they had escaped. So like life.

12. Phoebus means "bright" in Greek.

14. Eos is Aurora, the dawn.

15. Nox is a very ancient goddess, to whom only black animals were sacrificed.

18. Eurus is the wind from the east. "Are you soundly sure?" indicates anagram of "sure" + "u" sound = Eurus.

B6 *Taberna rustica*

The moving Latin inscription for which you were seeking is: *Ore stabit fortis arare placeto restat.* This comes out at "O rest a bit! For 'tis a rare place to rest at." You were warned...

Notes

1 across. *Pudor* means "shame"—nearly "sham".

11. Silver is *ag*, + I = *agi*.

8 down. "Soul ff (perhaps)"—an anagram of *sufflo*.

17. The Circus Maximus (c. 700 yards by 130 yards) with its twelve

starting-gates and seven-circuit races was the main site of the vastly popular chariot races in Rome (often staged by emperors to win favor). The four main teams were red, white, green and blue. We hear of a carrier-pigeon service to outlying towns, their legs painted suitably to match the color of the winners!

B7 Aquila musca

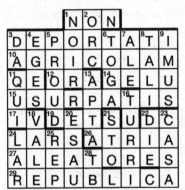

The triple acrostic spells out the Latin proverb *aquila non captat muscas*, "The eagle does not capture flies."

B8 State mottoes III

Notes

9 across. Ur was an ancient city of Sumeria south of Babylon, now in Southern Iraq. The whole of the region, called Mesopotamia (Greek, "in between the rivers", i.e. the Tigris and Euphrates), is known as the "cradle of civilization" because of the astonishing technological developments that took place there from c. 6000 BC onwards, e.g. the cultivation of cereals, olive and wine, pottery, copper-, bronze- and iron-working, writing, and so on, all to be picked up and transmitted down to

future generations all over the Mediterranean.

45. *sine aetate* appears on tombstones.

12 down. *Re mel* confused, yielding Merle (Oberon is husband of Titania in *Midsummer Night's Dream*).

20. *sine prole*, a tombstone abbreviation.

25. *Recto* (sc. *folio*) is the right-hand page of a book, abbreviated to r°.

26. *Miser* is half "miserable".

31. IHS = the first three letters of the Greek for Jesus in capital letters (IHSOUS in full, *Iêsous*).

37. "To our ears", antic sounds like "antique".

47. "Just a sec" is the same as "Half a mo[ment]".

B9 Shades in Hades

All the words in shaded squares are connected with the underworld:

Rivers: Lethe ("Forgetfulness"), Acheron, Styx ("Hateful")

Judges: Rhadamanthus; Minos; Aeacus.

Mortals punished: Tantalus (with food and drink always "tantalisingly" out of reach); Tityus (staked out while vultures ate his liver); Sisyphus (ordered to roll a rock over a hill, and always reaching the very top before it rolled back again).

Gods/goddesses: Pluto (= Hades, Greek *Ploutos*, "Wealth", because the underworld is rich in dead?); Hecate (hellish goddess of night); Nemesis ("retribution"); Hades ("unseen"); Otus (a giant).

Underworld: Hades; Orcus (Latin "underworld", and god of the dead).

In the absence of religious dogma (no church or bible: ancient religion was a matter of traditional ritual, not belief), there were as many views of the afterlife as there were writers about it.

B10 Lightweight country god

The three unclued words were Juno and Zeus, residing on Olympus.

The addition of the letters J and Z means that the grid contains all the letters of the alphabet—to make the grid a Pangram. Now look at the title of the puzzle. Lightweight—a gram; god of the country— Pan. Tortuous, or what?

Notes

3 across. Anagram of "squared up".

21. *Ritus*, a religious observance, was commonly used in the ablative form *ritu* in this sense.

3 down. "Flaming" hints at anagram of BarBque, mom (underlined B omitted).

4. "Unjustly" points to anagram of "claimed", but missing "m" for millions.

7. *Sextarius* was one-sixth of a *congius*, equal to about six pints, or one eighth of an *amphora*.

17. Plautus' *Mostellaria* is about a haunted house.

C1 Author, author!

The authors are (A) Plautus, (B) Caesar, (C) Suetonius, (D) Catullus, (E) Juvenal, (F) Lucretius, (G) Ovid, (H) Horace, (I) Tacitus, (J) Cicero, (K) Terence, (L) Virgil.

The author who will not fit into the puzzle is Catullus.

Notes

19 across. 'denied *in a muddle*' points to 'denied' as an anagram.

7 down. *Caesar* may be connected with *caesaries*, 'with red, or flowing, hair'—ironic, in that Julius Caesar at any rate spent much time trying to disguise his baldness. "Heard deed" is an anagram.

C2 *Ecce*! A palindrome!

The palindrome reads *In girum imus noctes, et consumimur igni*, "We go round in a circle at nights, and are consumed by fire".

Notes

E19 Om, the sacred syllable chanted by Buddhists.

F22 The *lectica* was a sort of sedan chair, in which slaves carried their masters. The emperor Claudius' came equipped with a gambling section.

iv4 Ur was an ancient Sumerian city (southern Iraq).

vi17 Latin letters often start '*X salutem (plurimam) dat Y*' lit. 'X gives (much) greeting to Y', shortened to '*X sd(p) Y*'.

vii7 The opening of a student drinking song. Similar to *Carmina Burana* (a set of 13th century songs, found in the Benedictine monastery at Beuern, whence *Burana*, in 1803 and set to music by Carl Orff in 1937).

C3 The missing emperor

C4 Whodunnit?

The clues were swan, Leda, Castor and Pollux, and the guilty party Zeus is hidden in the diagonal.

C5 Howlers

Notes

The crossword contained the following sayings, with their proper Latin translation:

Fiat lux—Let there be light
Ad hoc—To suit the occasion
Post hoc propter hoc—After this, on account of this
Carpe diem—Pluck the day
Rara avis—A rare bird
Noli me tangere—Do not touch me
Hic iacet—Here lies
Ars longa, vita brevis—Art is long, life short
Mens sana—A healthy mind
Summa cum laude—With the highest praise
Inter alia—Among other things

C6 Silver and gold

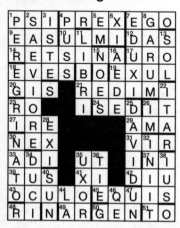

The deeply classical conundrum runs: *Si rex Midas in auro sedit, quis in argento?* "If King Midas sat on gold, who (sat) on silver?"

Wait for it: that horse shape in the middle of the crossword...the acrostic from 1-48 and 13-38 giving *peregrinator solitarius*...right, Tonto, it's the Lone Ranger.

Well, you were warned.

Notes

17 across. "Our mixture"—anagram of "our".

18. Eve is the first lady; eve is poetic for "evening".

19. Also spelled *exsul*.

23. See *Note* to B8 25d.

2 down. "Wildly" points to an anagram of "ie rave so".

8. *Garum*, wildly popular, was a sauce made of the intestines of mackerel or anchovies (or tuna, giving an even stronger flavor), macerated in salt and left out in the sun to decompose. Aromatic herbs were added, and a strainer used to collect the liquid, which was then left to mature. It was fantastically powerful, requiring only a drop or two to affect the taste of, e.g., a soup. It was also diluted with water, wine, oil and vinegar.

38. *ius* means law, justice, right (giving us words like "jury"); but the same letters form a different word, meaning soup or broth, giving us "juice".

C7 Delay* not

The missing word is *amor*, "love". Virgil wrote at *Eclogues* x. 69 *omnia vincit amor, et nos cedamus amori*, "Love conquers all, so let us too yield to love". Hence "Delay* not!" —"delay" in Latin being *mora*, an anagram of *amor* (not *mora*!).

Oh dear, is there no end to these appalling subtleties? No. Stop moaning and get on with your puzzles.

The Beatles' song at 23, 24, 25 is "All you need is love", or perhaps "a stiff drink" in this case.

Notes

10 across. The emperor Claudius, who was a keen writer of history, was fed poisoned mushrooms by his wife Agrippina in AD 54 to ensure that her son, Nero, succeeded to the imperial purple.

11. *quem* = "whom", 49 = IL.

14. Laomedon was a legendary king of Troy, famous for his treachery, who persuaded Apollo and Poseidon to build the walls of Troy, but then refused to pay them.

3 down. Neapolis is today Naples. Neapolis is Greek for "New City", it having been founded by Greek colonists c. 600 BC.

5. *Ioeidês* is Greek for "violet-like".

17. Niobe was turned into stone for boasting she had more children that Leto (mother of Artemis and Apollo).

18. "Sabine" is an anagram of "is bane" (no!). When in their earliest years Romans needed to populate Rome, they invited the women of the Sabines, a neighboring tribe, to a show and seized them as wives.

C8 In Kansas

When a whirlwind, *turbo*, hit her farm, *Dorothea* accompanied by Toto met up with the Tin Woodsman, *Lignator Stanneus*, the Cowardly Lion, *Leo Ignavus*, and the Scarecrow, *Terriculus*, and together they set off down. the Yellow—that was your bit—Brick Road, *Via Latericia*, to see (*ut viderent*) the Wonderful Wizard, *Magus Mirabilis*, of OZ.

C9 Proverbs II

Festina lente, "More haste, less speed" (lit. "Hasten slowly").

Qualis pater, talis filius, "Like father, like son."

Non omne quod nitet aurum est, "All that glitters is not gold."

Finis coronat opus, "All's well that ends well" (lit. "The finish crowns the work").

Bis dat qui cito dat, "A friend in need is a friend indeed" (lit. "he gives twice who gives immediately").

Verba non alunt familiam, "Fine words butter no parsnips" (lit. "Words do not feed a household").

Notes

1 across. Scipio Africanus defeated the Carthaginian Hannibal at Zama in north Africa in 202 BC. Sixteen years earlier, Hannibal had invaded Italy with elephants.

14. Nestor was king of "sandy Pylos" in Homer. The town has been excavated: it is near Navarino Bay in south-western Greece.

22. *Cicuta* is Latin for "hemlock" (botanical term *conium maculatum*).

35. Cf. Czar (or Tsar).

46. From *enascor*.

38. *Labor*, "work" = "lab" + "or" ("no alternative" follows!).

C10 Rigorous limerick

The limerick reads:

Puella Rigensis ridebat
Quam tigris in tergo vehebat.
  Externa profecta
  Interna revecta,
Sed risus in tigre manebat.

"There was a young lady of Riga
Who went for a ride on a tiger.
  They returned from the ride
  With the lady inside
And a smile on the face of the tiger."

Notes

42 across. "I trot" is an anagram of *trito* (*tero*).

44. "I forgot", i.e. the letter *i* omitted from "tunic".

17 down. SLP = *sine legali prole*.

20. *Sesquipes* = one and a half *pes*. *Semis* + *que* = *sesque* = one and a half times.

34. "In place where" indicates that the letters of the next words contain the answer: "met Ron" = *metron*.

D1 Birds, wasps, clouds, frogs

Notes

The crossword title consists of the names of plays by Aristophanes.

24 across. "Short *rex*" = r; "possessed a chap" = had a man; *ita* = thus.

1 down. Argus was sent by Hera to spy on her husband Zeus's lover Io (whom Zeus had turned into a cow). When Hermes killed him, Hera transferred his hundred eyes to the peacock's tale.

2. Icarus, son of Daedalus, flew too near the sun.

4. The lighthouse of Pharos was one of the seven wonders of the ancient world.

5. Tacitus tells how Nero tried to kill his mother Agrippina by means of an accident at sea. When it failed and she swam ashore, Nero sent Anicetus and some men to find and kill her. Her last words were "Strike my womb!"

12. After the death of Alexander the Great in 323 BC, Seleucus, one of his generals, became the Greek king of Babylonia and nearby regions.

16. Museum is in fact the Greek *Mouseion*, home of the (nine) Muses, goddesses of culture.

D2 Agnew's hope

Motto: *Dum spiro, spero* "While I breathe, I hope"

Notes

8 across. Bulbus, possessing nothing (o), = "bulbous".

11. Comets get their name from Greek *komêtês*, "with hair" (rather than our "tails").

D3 The seven hills of Rome

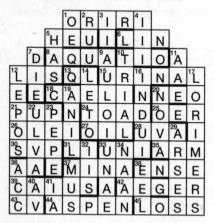

The Seven Hills of Rome can be seen marked in mountain shapes in the grid.

Notes

10/23 across. Sherry, of which Tio Pepe is a brand, derives from the

Caesaris [urbs], Caesar's [city], a town in Spain. *Caesaris* became Xeres, which became Jerez and so sherry.

15. *Urna* + LI.

20. Neo = new; and one (made new) is an anagram of neo.

25. *Remus*—"oar"; "all up with" = "over"; poetically, "o'er".

26. "Olé" plus i = *olei*, "of oil".

30. RSVP, without French "reply", = SVP.

37. Greek *mina* or *mna* was a coin, worth 100 drachmae.

39. Gaius, or (softer) Caius, Julius Caesar.

1 down. "Oi", reverse of Greek *io*.

29. *Thesis* and *arsis* are the technical terms for down.- and up-beat in verse, the lowering and raising of the foot (in the physical and metrical sense).

32. "If one" = *si I* (Latin numeral); "rises" = backwards = *iis* "for them".

34. "Whichever way you look"—"naan" is a palindrome.

D4 Hanging by a thread

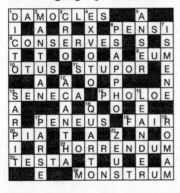

Notes

1 across. Damocles, envious of the tyrant Dionysius' life, was invited to try it, and found himself sitting on a couch surrounded by luxuries but with a sword hanging by a thread over him.

6. "In open site".

11. Frederick II (1194-1250), Holy Roman Emperor, was known as the *stupor mundi* for his immense learning.

17. "Quietly" = *p*(iano).

15 down. Leander swam the Hellespont every night to reach his mistress Hero on the other side. One night he was drowned, and Hero drowned herself in sympathy. Lord Byron tried the trick, but only caught a cold.

D5 Slander at the opera

Notes

10 across. Pro-pontis is (literally) "in front of" Pontus = Greek *pontos* = sea = Black Sea.

3 down. The Trojan horse, of course, left by "departing" Greeks as an offering to the gods, but containing Greek soldiers.

5. The Bandusian spring was on Horace's farm, and he annually stained its bright, bubbling waters with the blood of a goat-sacrifice.

16. The *lictores* attended the magistrates (top elected executive officials, like praetors and consuls) carrying the *fasces*, a bundle of rods with an axe in the middle, as a sign of the magistrates' authority (*imperium*—the right to give orders).

21. "in Gaul anywhere". *Aula* is a Greek word, used of the courts of Greek kings. It was hardly used in Latin before the period of the Roman emperors—the new "kings" of Rome, after the break-up of the republic.

D6 Enigma variations

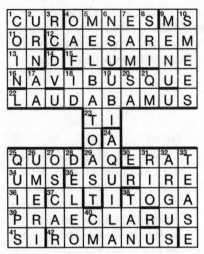

Q: *Cur omnes Caesarem in flumine navibusque laudabamus?* "Why did we all praise Caesar in the river and on boats?"
A: *Quod erat praeclarus Romanus!* "Because he was a famous Roman!"

Get it? No? We are in full sympathy. Prepare yourself. "Row-man"… The drinks cabinet is on the left. Go for it.

Notes

23 across. Ti is a note in the tonic sol-fa.
4 down. Anagram of "of a".

D7 Watch your pelvis

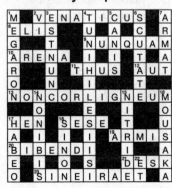

Notes

8 across. Elis (anagram of "isle") was the small town near Olympia (which was one vast sanctuary, lacking nearly all facilities for spectators) which ran the games every four years.

17. Sacred hens were offered food, and if they ate, the omens were good. Before one important sea-battle, they refused, and the general hurled them into the water, exclaiming "If they will not eat, let

them drink!" He lost.

20.   Horace said *nunc est bibendum*—"Now drinking is necessary."

6 down. "Round" indicates anagram formed by "about" = c + "statue".

18.   Sinon (*si non*) was the Greek "abandoned" when the Greeks "left" Troy to persuade the Trojans to bring the Wooden Horse inside the citadel.

D8 Vegetable spy

Notes

8 across. Pilumnus was so-called because of his invention of the pestle, *pilum*, for crushing corn.

9.   Philomela ("mope a hill") was seduced by Tereus, who was married to her sister Procne. To do this, Tereus persuaded Philomela that Procne was dead, and then cut out her tongue so that she could not tell Procne what had happened when she found Procne was still alive.

13.   Uranus (Greek *Ouranos*, "Sky") was castrated by Cronus on the orders of Uranus' wife Gaia. Aphrodite was born from his semen when it fell foaming on the sea.

21.   "Erin" is a poetic name for Ireland. "Indeed" = yes.

D9 X marks the spot—the great adventure

	1	2	3	4	5	6	7	8	9	10	11	12
A	J	A	S	O	N	A	C	A	S	T	U	S
B	S	P	I	R	A	M	L	I	N	O	N	I
C	E	T	S	A	T	B	O	V	E	S	I	D
D	T	A	N	G	I	O	D	I	F	O	V	A
E	U	M	E	R	O			L	A	C	E	S
F	B	A	S	E		L	E		S	E	R	T
G	R	E	N	D		E	D		O	R	S	I
H	E	D	E	I	C		E	C	S	I	P	
I	G	I	T	E	H	E	N	S	N	A	I	H
J	A	S	T	R	O	L	O	G	U	S	R	Y
K	E	C	I	E	R	L	E	O	N	R	U	S
L	L	E	M	N	O	I	L	A	C	U	E	D

Jason led *Acastus*, *Idas*, *Tiphys*, *Deucalion*, *Meleager*, and *Butes* in search of the *Golden Fleece*.

Notes

B12-10 Ino saved Odysseus when a storm smashed his ship.

G9-12 *Orsi* = or ("alternative") + is "back" (i.e. reversed).

K6-9 The stem of *leo* is *leon-*.

4A-C *Aro* "up" = *ora*.

4F-D "Therefore" = *ergo*; "loveless" = no "o".

D10 Up, up and away

Notes

10 across. Attic, adjective from Attica, the territory of which Athens was the main city.

16. The Greek *a*-prefix indicates negative; *pod-* = foot (cf. Latin *pes*).

21. etc. "Nagging"—"black care" sits behind the rider on a nag.

26. *Mus + Lar +* cu "at the heart", i.e. in the middle.

3 down. "Us" + "Ares" somehow (anagram) = "assure".

29. "It's a"—anagram.

E1 Fairground warning

Notes

1 across. Calliope = call (summon) + Io + PE (= physical education). Calliope, daughter of Jupiter and Mnemosyne ("memory"), was represented with a trumpet in her right hand and scrolls in her left.

9. Niobe was the daughter of Tantalus and wife of Amphion. She was turned to stone, weeping for her slaughtered children. See Notes on puzzle C7 at 17d.

10. Publius Ovidius Naso ("Big Nose") was a Roman poet born in Sulmo in 43BC who died in exile at Tomis (Constanta, Romania) on the Black Sea. Ted Hughes's *Tales from Ovid* is a recreation of his very influential *Metamorphoses*.

12. Anagram of "trite".

18/5. *Absit omen*, "May it not be an omen." Romans were as superstitious as we are.

20. "The greatest respect is owed to a boy." Juvenal stresses the innocence of childhood—very apposite today in a world of youth clamouring to grow up.

21. Decurio is hidden in "blockade curious". The decurio commanded a *decuria*, a body of ten men, technically one tenth of a century and a thirtieth of a legion. The term was also used of a local councillor.

24. Dio (Cassius) was an ancient historian; an ancient Persian people were the Medes. Diomedes was one of the bravest of Greek chiefs at Troy.

2 down. Laocoon was a Trojan priest, the son of Priam and Hecuba. He made a sacrifice to see if the Wooden Horse was friendly or not. Serpents at once emerged from the sea and attacked his sons; he died trying to save them.

4. "It is sweet and seemly/proper to die for one's country."

6. John Major, the British Prime Minister after Mrs Thatcher and before Mr Blair.

15. *Thebaid*—one (= i) in "the bad". The *Thebaid* was an epic about Thebes that took Statius twelve years to write. It told of the war between the Thebans and the Argives.

17. Bootes is a constellation in the northern sky near Ursa Major.

19. "So" + cci.

20. "I" in "pram", short for perambulator. Priam was the last King of Troy, killed by Achilles' son Neoptolemus before his throne/altar in a gloriously futile but heroic attempt to avenge the death of his son Polites.

E2 Word-square

	A	B	C	D	E	F	G	H	I
I	¹I	²A	³M	⁴P	⁵R	⁶I	⁷D	⁸E	⁹M
II	¹⁰O	V	E	R	E	T	I	P	I
III	¹¹N	E	R	O	T	A	S	I	S
IV	¹²E	X	O	P	E	R	A	S	C
V	¹³P	E	T	E	N	E	T	T	E
VI	¹⁴A	R	A	R	E	P	O	U	A
VII	¹⁵S	U	S	A	T	O	R	L	M
VIII	¹⁶O	N	E	N	U	N	D	A	U
IX	¹⁷S	T	A	T	I	O	N	E	S

stationes

Word Chains

I. I am *iam*/amp/pride/*idem* = *iampridem*

II. *O ver*!over/*vere*/*et*/tip/pi

III. Nero/*rotas*/as is

IV. ex/*exo*/op/per/*eras*/sc

V. pet/*pete*/tene/net/TT/te

VI. *ara*/*arare*/repo/ou/ua

VII. *sus*/USA/*sat*/to/tor/RL/LM

VIII. one/*en*/nun/und/*unda*/au

IX. st/*stat*/ti/io/ones =

A. *io*/ion/*nepa*/as/so/os/SOS

B. ave/ex/vexer/run/runt = *avexerunt*

C. mer/*mero*/rot/TA/as/sea

D. pro/prope/per/era/ant/erant = *properant*

E. re/et/te/rete/ten/tene/*tenet*/tu/tui

F. it/*ita*/tare/ep/Po/O no! = *repono*

G. di/*Dis*/sat/to/or/rd/dn

H. epi/pis/st/tu/ul(n)a/ae = *epistulae*

I. mis/SC/CE/eam/mus = *misceamus*

Word-square

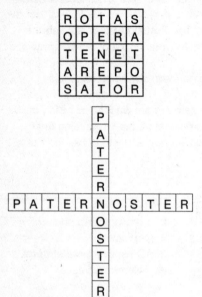

The Cirencester word-square (it was found at Cirencester, in the UK) may mean "Arepo [an Anglo-Saxon name] the ploughman holds the wheels with exertion/as a hired hand".

Word games have always been popular but words have also been considered to have hidden power. This word-square may be of Christian origin. Twenty-one letters of the square make up *Pater Noster*, "Our Father", twice (sharing the N in common), rather like the Paternoster cross. That leaves four other letters, A and O—also twice (alpha and omega).

E3 What is truth?

Notes

1/13/2/11 across. *Quot homines, tot sententiae*, said by the Roman playwright Terence, lit. "How many men—so many opinions".

8.   *Ôt-* is the stem of the Greek for "ear".

14.   Greek *scholê* means "leisure", the origin of Latin *schola* and our "school", to which (originally) only the leisurely rich could go.

18. Tempe was a valley in Thessaly between Mt. Olympus to the north and Mt. Ossa to the south through which the river Peneus flowed into the Aegean. It was the ancient equivalent of an unspoilt paradise, and the river was said to contain speaking trout.

20. "You are that" = *id* + *es* = Ides, the 13th–15th of the month, and in March the date of the assassination of Julius Caesar

23. Dido with no love (o) = did = *fecit*. Dido was Queen of Carthage who, according to Virgil, committed suicide after the Roman hero Aeneas abandoned her. This was the origin of the hatred between Rome and Carthage (hence the Punic wars).

24. Zeus, in the form of a swan, seduced Leda.

28. *Stet* = "let it stand". It is still used as an instruction in manuscript correction.

3 down. The answer to a prayer or vow offered up to the gods for successful completion. 'votum'—vow, prayer, votive offering.

4. *Ex pede Herculem*: "You can tell the size of Hercules from his footprint." This was 6ft 7in according to Pythagoras, who worked it out from the size of the Olympic stadium, supposedly measured by the hero's foot.

25. Dis, cf. B 9.

E4 Screen *stellae*

Clark Fastigium (Gable)
Re vera, cara mea, flocci non facio
Frankly, my dear, I don't give a damn
James Cagney
Tu rattus, tu rattus turpis!
You rat, you dirty rat!
Clint Silvaorientalis (Eastwood)
Age! Fac ut gaudeam !
Go ahead! Make my day!
To Ossa McCoy
Me transmitte sursum, Caledoni!
Beam me up, Scotty!
Mae Occidens (West)
Interdum ascende, ut me visas

Come up and see me sometime
About Christophoro Reeve
Estne avis? Estne aeronavis? Non. Supervir est
Is it a bird? Is it a plane? No. It's Superman.

Notes

16 across. "Wild" indicates that "riots" is an anagram.
26. Asa is the Hebrew name for healer = a + *as* (Roman coin).
45. "Broken" indicates that "nib"is an anagram.
24 down.   *Os* "bone" reversed = "so" = *ita*, *sic*.
30. Na is the abbreviation for sodium.
37. "Moving around" indicates an anagram of a rat-t, *artat* "(s)he curtails".

E5 Roscius' boar

Notes

1 across. Thespis, a sixth-century BC Athenian poet and supposed inventor of tragedy. Roscius in the puzzle's title was a Roman actor, defended by Cicero in an extant speech.
8. "Horrible" indicates an anagram of "cameo".
11. An owl symbolised wisdom, epitomised by Minerva/Athena.
15. "Reportedly" indicates that the answer sounds like " 'e shaved"—i.e. " 'e rased".
20. "Stir up" indicates an anagram of "tea/rest".
22. Susa is hidden in "matchless USA". Susa, now Suster, was the winter capital of the mighty Persian Empire (Ecbatana was the summer capital).
1/18 down. *O tempora, o mores* was Cicero's comment on the failure of the Roman senate to act decisively over the rebellion of Catiline.

2. "Sounds like X L" = "excel".

3. "Frantically" indicates an anagram of "is pale" + "routs". Protesilaus was the first of the Greeks to set foot on the Trojan shore, and was therefore doomed by an oracle to die. His wife Laodamia killed herself on hearing of his death.

6. "Fatality" indicates an anagram of "or crisp". Procris, daughter of Erectheus, the king of Athens, married Cephalus and, wrongly suspecting him of infidelity, was accidentally killed by him as she spied on him during a hunt.

7. "Comical" indicates an anagram of "sir it".

14. "Likely to collapse" indicates an anagram of "stonier". Neritos was a mountain on Ithaca, island home of Odysseus.

E6 In Wonderland

Notes

Who (qui) is she? She is Alice (3ac) in *Terra Mirabili* [Wonderland]. After the waves [*undae*] of the *stagnum lacrimarum* [Pool of Tears], she met the *cuniculus albus* [White Rabbit]. On a *boletus* [mushroom] sat an *eruca* [caterpillar] with a *tubulo tabaci* [hookah]. In the *culina* [kitchen] of the duchess [*ducissa*] an

infans [baby] turned into a *sus* [pig]. She saw in an *arbore* [tree] the *feles Cestriana* [Cheshire cat] with a *risus* [smile] that left behind only a *rictus* [grin]. Around the *mensa* [table] were gathered the *Lepus Martius* [March Hare], *Venditor petasi demens* [Mad Hatter], the *glis* [dormouse], a sort of *mus* [mouse]. The *regina* [Queen] was playing a *lusus* [game] that needed a *phoenicopter* [flamingo] and an *ericius* [hedgehog]. On the edge *orae* [of the shore] was a *dodo* [Dodo] but it ended in court with the *rex, regina, baro* [King, Queen, Knave] *cordium* [of Hearts].

27 across. *Nostri* = "Our men" sounds like "amen".

34.   16 = "Ha" + "wild" (= mixed up) ox = hoax.

44.   Ean means "bring forth, give birth to", an anagram of "E" + "an".

46.   "Neither" = *neu* + "nor" reversed.

60.   "She was"* = *erat* + "o" (love) = Erato, a muse.

74.   "Foreign" indicates anagram of "aid".

77.   "Eclipsed" indicates anagram of "is sun", meaning "effort".

78.   "Poor" indicates anagram of "a diet".

85.   "From" indicates anagram of E gardener, but not "r".

36 down. D + "in".

38.   "Mo"(ment) is a short time + "urn" = mourn.

43.   "Unio" is a pearl = *uni* ("for one") + round ("o").

48.   Up + r + l = purl (flow gently).

52.   *Dromos* is a Greek racecourse (cf. hippodrome); also an entrance to a subterranean tomb.

74.   "Strange" indicates anagram of "a bid".

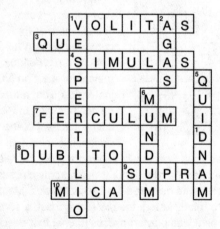

Mica, vespertilio,	Twinkle, twinkle, little bat,
Quidnam agas, dubito.	How I wonder what you're at.
supra mundum volitas	Up above the sky so high
ferculumque simulas.	Like a tea-tray in the sky.
	Ludovicius Carrollus

E7 In your hat

Notes

15 across. Gaels "sounds like" gales.

39.   Satyrs were demigods of the countryside, resembling men but with goat's feet/legs, short horns, and a hairy body. They were the chief attendants of Bacchus. Romans called them *Fauni*, *Panes*, or *Silvani*.

57.   Nais, one of the Oceanides, who in Ovid's *Metamorphoses* changed all her guests into fish suppers.

59. Urd is hidden in "sour dough".

And the, er, "Latin" poem? Yes, it's the old dog-Latin favorite about Caesar having some jam for tea while Brutus ate a rat, and where they were sick afterwards. Kids! Doncha love 'em?

> *Caesar adsum jam forte*
> *Brutus aderat;*
> *Caesar sic in omnibus*
> *Brutus inisat* (= in 'is 'at).

E8 Triplets

Notes

12 across. "Use" indicates anagram of "the car".

17. "Ill" indicates anagram, of "Iain" + "I" = *anili* (dative, "for").

19. *dolorosus* = "achy". "Sinking" indicates anagram of "yacht", with "t" for "time" missing.

25. Isaac [Ike] is the Hebrew word for "laugh" = *risus*.

28. *Ecce* = "Lo" + "u" (you, soundly) = Lou.

33. "Earlap" is an anagram of "a pearl".

19 down. Aeneas was the eponymous hero of Virgil's *Aeneid*, an epic poem in twelve books.

20. *Gnaeus Pompeius "Magnus"*, Pompey the Great, was an ally, then a rival, of Julius Caesar; defeated by Caesar in the Civil War beginning in 49 BC; and was finally assassinated in Egypt.

FATES were the goddesses of birth and death. Clotho was the youngest, presiding over birth holding a distaff; Lachesis spun out all the actions and events of life; Atropos was the eldest, cutting the thread of life with scissors.

GORGONS were three sisters with their hair entwined with serpents, hands of brass, scaly bodies, and teeth as long as wild boar's tusks. They had the power to turn anyone looking at them to stone. Only Medusa was mortal. In some versions of the myth they shared an eye and a tooth. Perseus slew Medusa (avoiding petrification by looking at her reflection in his shield) and gave her head to Athena/Minerva as the center of her terrifying aegis.

GRACES, *Charites* or *Gratiae*, were the three daughters of Jupiter and Eurynome and the constant attendants upon Venus.

HARPIES were winged monsters with the faces of women, the bodies of vultures, and fingers consisting of short claws.

The missing names can be found in the two diagonals—the blocked squares needing H, I, Y, A to complete them. The missing members of the trios are in capitals. They are: The three Fates—Clotho, Atropos and LACHESIS; the three Gorgons—Medusa, Stheno and EURYALE; the three Graces—Aglaia, Euphrosyne and THALIA; and the three Harpies—Aello, Celeno and OCYPETE.

There are no prizes for constructing a crossword featuring modern Fates, Gorgons, Graces and Harpies. There are far too many possibilities.

E9 Christmas I: from oxen to pears

The introduction reads:
duodecima die natalis amator dedit mi "On the twelfth day of Christmas my true love gave to me".

Now you can sing in Latin:
Duodecima die natalis amator dedit mi
d'odecim qui pulsant,
undecim tibic'nes,
decem salt'tores,

novem salt'trices,
octo quae mulgent,
septem cygnos nantes,
sex anseres,
quinque anulos,
quattuor aves,
tres gallinas,
d'os turtures
et perdicem in piro.

Notes

A. C. "Wild" indicates anagram of "oats".

34. "In need of repairing" indicates anagram of "one".

12d. *apud* = "a pud" (ChriStmas pudDing).

29. "Aroused" indicates anagram of "tell on".

E10 Christmas II: Rufus

Here is the whole song:

Rufe, nasute cerve,	Rufus, the nosy reindeer,
Nasus tuus ruber stat.	Your nose stands out red.
Immo, si vera dicam,	Indeed, if I tell the truth,
Nasus tuus conflagrat.	Your nose is on fire.
Omnes ad unum cervi	All reindeer to a deer
Eum risu lacerant.	Hurt him with their laughter.
Misero Rufo numquam	To miserable Rufus never
Lascivire secum dant.	Did they grant [permission] to play with them.
Nebuloso vesperi	On a cloudy evening
Venit Iuppiter:	Jupiter came:
"Rufe, nitido vultu,	"Rufus, with the glowing face,
Nonne Iovem trahes tu?"	Surely you will pull Jove?"
Illum nunc amant omnes.	Now they all love him.
Audi quam clamaverint:	Listen how they shout:
"Rufe, nasute cerve,	"Rufus, nosy reindeer,
Omnes te meminerint!"	Everyone will remember you!"

Appendix: The pronunciation of Latin and the spelling of Greek[1]

The pronunciation of Latin arouses fierce passions. Many people assert that no one knows how it was pronounced, and then argue that Latin *v* was pronounced as English "v", not "w". Others say that Latin *in caelis*, "in the heavens", should be pronounced "in chaylees", not "in kylees".

Arguments about pronunciation and grammar existed in fifth-century BC Athens. Modern pronunciations of Latin exist for a variety of reasons. There is the old French pronunciation, dating back to AD 1066. After William Duke of Normandy's conquest of England, Latin was taught with a French pronunciation. Hence *gens*, "tribe", was pronounced "jens", *iustus*, "just", was pronounced "justus", *Cicero* (hard *c*) as "Sisero". Then there is the revised pronunciation of the great Dutch scholar Erasmus, published in 1528, and expounded in an agreeable discussion between a bear and a lion. This never fully caught on, but was itself subject to corruption because of the change of pronunciation in English: thus in the course of the Great Vowel Shift, long *i*, "ee", became pronounced as in "wine". Then again, there is church pronunciation, which is nothing but the modern Italian that Pope Pius X tried to impose on the church in 1912 (hence "chaylees").

The debate has surfaced intermittently on and off, but was finally laid to rest in 1965 when W. S. Allen, Professor of Comparative Philology at Cambridge University, published his definitive *Vox Latina: The Pronunciation of Classical Latin* (Cambridge: 1965; revised 1989). He concludes "The degree of accuracy with which we can reconstruct the ancient pronunciation varies from sound to sound, but for the most part can be determined within quite narrow limits." The evidence is impressive and wide-ranging. Here are a few examples and the conclusions they lead to:

1 Writers talk about the how the language sounded. Thus the grammarian Terentianus Maurus talks of the vibrating sound the Latin *r* produced, and the satirist Lucilius says that *r* sounds like a growling dog. This means we should trill *r* (as the Scots do) in Latin, thus distinguishing

---

1 This appendix is taken from Peter Jones, *An Intelligent Person's Guide to Classics* (Duckworth 1999).

cl

between *pacis*, "of peace", and *parcis*, "you spare".

2 The transliteration of Latin into other languages yields important results. We know that ancient Greek *k* was pronounced hard. So when Latin *Cicero* appears in Greek as *Kikerôn* and not *Siserôn* (the –*ôn* ending is a Greek termination), we can be certain that Latin *c* was pronounced hard. In time, it softened (Latin for "hundred", *centum*, becomes French *cent*), but our evidence suggests this did not happen until about AD 500.

3 Meter helps the argument. Take the pronunciation of Latin *v*. The word "wood", *silva*, appears occasionally in verse as three syllables. If *v* was pronounced "w", this would explain why this should be ("sil-oow-a"); with *v* pronounced as "v", *silva* could never be scanned as three syllables. Then again *Valerius* appears transliterated into Greek as *Oualerios*, suggesting the "w" sound; and a Latin grammarian argued that when you said *tu* ("you" singular) and *vos* ("you" plural) in Latin, your lips pointed at the person you were addressing. This would happen only if *v* was pronounced "w". So however much the words may sound to us like characters from the Seven Dwarfs, Julius Caesar did indeed say "wayny, weedy, weeky" (*veni, vidi, vici*, "I came, I saw, I conquered"). Over time *v* changed its sound, and a Latin grammarian of the second century AD tells us it was pronounced "with friction". That suggests it was now sounding more like "v".

4 Inscriptions are extremely informative, especially when they are incorrect. For example, we find *in pace*, "in peace", written *im pace*, and *in balneo*, "in the bath", as *im balneo*. So it looks as if Romans slurred "n" to "m" before a "p" or a "b". Even more surprising, we find *ignes*, "fires", written as *ingnes*, and there is other evidence to suggest that "gn" was pronounced "ngn". So *magnus*, "large", sounded roughly like English "ha*ngn*ail".

5 Spelling conventions also help. *Consul*, "consul", was often written *cosul*, and when Romans abbreviated it, they wrote *cos.*, not *con.* or *cons.* So "n" was probably not pronounced before "s". Further evidence is supplied by ancient Greek, which writes the Latin name *Hortensius* as *Hortesios*; and we hear of aristocratic Romans like Cicero preferring to drop *n* before *s* and saying e.g. *foresia*, "public matters", not *forensia*. Cf. modern Italian "bride", *sposa*, with Latin *sponsa*, "spouse".

No language stands still. Ancient English was no more pronounced like modern English than Latin was like modern Italian, or ancient Greek like modern Greek (on which, see W. S. Allen, *Vox Graeca* [third edition, Cambridge: 1987]). On the other hand, one is free to pronounce a foreign language according to the conventions of the mother tongue (we do not pronounce "Paris", the capital of France, as the French do, nor "Cicero" as the Romans did). The pronunciation of Church Latin is now traditional. If it bears no relation to classical Latin, so what? But if one wants a common pronunciation, then classical Latin as described by Professor Allen offers a standard, in the same way that a Frenchman's French, rather than President Clinton's, does for that language.

The spelling of ancient Greek proper names in English causes similar problems, because Greek proper names have been adopted into English in their Latin forms, Latin having been the language of English education for so long. For example, Plato is the Latinised form of Greek *Platon*, Apollo of *Apollon*. The following examples indicate the basic rules of the Latinisation of Greek.[2] The Greek is exactly transliterated, and the Latin equivalent given in the next column:

GREEK	LATIN	NOTES
Thoukudidês	Thucydides	Greek *ou* becomes Latin *u*; Greek *u* becomes Latin *y*, in certain circumstances;[3] Greek *k* becomes Latin *c*.
Aiskhulos	Aeschylus	Greek *ai* becomes Latin *ae*; Greek *–os* ending becomes Latin *–us* ending. Thus Greek *Epikouros* becomes Latin *Epicurus*.
Ilion	Ilium	Greek *–on* ending becomes Latin *–um*.
Akhilleus	Achilles	Greek *–eus* ending becomes Latin *–es*.
Phoibê	Phoebe	Greek *–oi* can become Latin *–oe*.
Peirênê	Pirene	Greek *-ei* can become Latin *–i*.

Even so, that is not the end of the story, because English has its own conventions as well, which control the final English form of the Latinised

Greek word. For example, Greek *Korinthos*, Latin *Corinthus*, but English Corinth; Greek *Athenai*, Latin *Athenae*, but English Athens; Greek *Aristoteles*, so Latin, but English Aristotle, and so on.

2 It is worth saying here that Latin had no letters 'v' or 'j' – only 'u' and 'i'. The use of 'v' and 'j' in texts is an English convention.

3 Romans introduced *y* to replicate Greek *u* in the first century BC. *Y* was used only in words adopted from Greek. The same is true of Latin *z*. Neither is a 'natural' Roman letter.

Glossary

Accused: *reus*
Adligo: tie, bind
Aged: *aetate*
Agrestis: countryman
Alas!: *eheu, heu*
Alexandrian wonder: Pharos
All together: *universus*
Alone: *solus*
Always: *semper*
Anger: *ira*
Anguilla: eel
Ankles, dice: *tali*
Antigone's sister: Ismene
Anywhere: *alibi*
Apollo: Phoebus
Approach: *adeo, appropinquo*
Ara: altar
Arise: *orior*
Arm: *armo*
Arms: *arma*
As: small Roman coin
As: *ut*
Asinus: ass
Ask: *rogo*
Attract: *adlicio*
Augur's staff: *lituus*
Augustus' wife: Livia
Auris: ear
Aurunca: Suessa
Band of dancers: *chorus*
Bare: *nudus*
Be burnt up: *uror*
Bear: *ursus, ursa*
Bee: *apis*
Beef: *bubula*
Before: *ante*
Beget: *creo*
Beneath: *sub*

Berry: *baca*
Bird: *avis*
Black Sea entrance: Propontis
Black: *ater*
Body: *corpus*
Boletus: mushroom
Bone: *os*
Book: *liber*
Both: *ambo*
Branch: *ramus*
Brave: *fortis*
Breast: *mamma*
Bring: *fero*
Bufo: toad
Bull: *bos*
Burn: *uro*
Buy: *emo*
C: 100
Caespes: sod
Censor: Cato
Centaurs' home: Pholoe
Cerva: doe, hind
Cervus: deer
Charm: *lepos*
Cineres: ashes
Citadel: *arx*
Clavis: nail
Cobbler: *sutor*
Coil: *spira*
Coin (small): *as*
Contradict: *obloquor*
Cornix: crow
Cottage: *casa*
Count: *numero*
Countryside: *rus*
Courage, valor: *virtus*
Court: *aula*
Crawl: *repto, serpo*
Cronus' father: Uranus

Cross-divide: *decusso*
Crus: leg
Cry of joy, despair: *io*
Cuttlefish: *sepia*
D: 500
Damnum: loss
Dancing-place: *orchestra*
Date: *palma*
Dawn: Eos
Day: *dies*
Decide: *statuo*
Delay: *tardo*
Desert: *desero*
Destroy: *deleo*
Diana: Artemis
Dives: rich
Divided: *separatus*
Doctor: *medicus*
Dog: *canis*
Drink: *bibo*
Drive, do: *ago*
Duly, properly: *rite, ritu*
Dunce, knave: *baro*
Dutiful: *pius*
Eagle: *aquila*
Eat: *edo*
Ebriosus: drunk
Egg: *ovum*
Egypt, sacred bird: *ibis*
Elm: *ulmus*
Enough: *satis, sat*
Enrich: *dito*
Enter: *ineo*
Epigrammatist: Martial(*is*)
Even, too: *etiam*
Eye: *oculus*
Farewell!: *vale*
Farmer: *agricola*

Fasces: bundles of rods and an axe, carried by *lictor*
Father-in-law: *socer*
Feed: *alo*
Feles: cat
Fierce: *saevus*
Fish sauce: *garum*
Fish: *piscis*
Flowering bush: *rosa*
Flower-nymph: Acantha
Fold, bay: *sinus*
Follow: *sequor*
Foot-and-a-half: *sesquipes*
For a long time: *diu*
Force: *vis*
Fourth: *quartus*
Frequento: haunt
Frog: *rana*
Fucus: rouge
Furies: *Erinyes*
Gallina: hen
Gambler: *aleator*
Gape, yawn: *hio*
Ghosts (of dead): *lemures*
Giants: Otus and Ephialtes
Gift of god: Theodore
Gingiva: gum
Give: *do*
Glacies: ice
Glaeba: clod, sod
Go away: *abeo*
Go out: *exeo*
Go: *eo*
God: *deus*: pl. *di* or *dei*; f. *dea*;
   of harvest, Ceres;
   of war, Ares, Mars;

of underworld, Persephone;
of household, Lar, Penates;
of country, Pales;
of bakers, Pilumnus;
of wealth, Ops;
of travellers, Hermes;
of disaster: *Atê*;
Egyptian sun-god, Ra;
Egyptian goddess, Isis
Gold: *aurum*
Goose: *anser*
Grape: *uva*
Gratitude: *gratia*
Greek pipes: *auloi*
Greek traitor: Sinon
Ground: *solum*
Guard: *custos*
Guardian of Io: Argus
Hall, Greek: *megaron*
Hallway: *atrium*
Hannibal: defeated at Zama
Hate: *odi*
Heart: *cor*
Herba: grass
Hey!: *heus*
Honey: *mel*
Hope: *spes*
Horace: wrote *Odes*
Horse: *equus*
Humorous: *iocosus*
Hungry, be: *esurio*
Hunter-constellation: Orion
Hunting: *venaticus*
Idem ac: the same as

In order to: *ut*
Inborn: *innatus*
Incense: *tus, thus*
Increase: *cresco*
Instruo: draw up
Invented: *fictus*
Ita vero: yes, indeed
Javelin: *pilum*
Judge of underworld: Rhadamanthus
Know: *scio*
L: 50
Lack, need, want: *egeo*
Law, soup: *ius*
Lead: *duco*
Leader: *dux*
Learn: *disco*
Lectica: carriage, sedan-chair
Life: *vita*
Look! See! Lo and behold!: *ecce, en*
Low down: *imus*
Ludibrio habere: tease
M: 1000
Maintain: *conservo*
Make a mistake: *erro*
Make thin: *extenuo*
Measure, method: *modus*
Milk: *lac*
Mistress: *era*
Mouse: *mus*
Move: *moveo*
Multiply: *multiplicor*
Murder, death: *nex*
Naxos: *Dia*
Nero's henchman: Anicetus
Nero's tutor: Seneca
Nettle: *urtica*
Never: *numquam*

Note: sol-fa, doh, etc.
Now: *nunc, iam*
Nundinae: fair
Obturamentum: plug
Ocellus: eye
Of account: *pensi*
Olea: olive (oil)
Oleum: oil
Olympic Games: held at Elis
On account of: *ob*: *propter*
One: *unus*
Or: *aut*
Ornament and protection: *decus et tutamen*
Outstanding: *insignis*
Owe: *debeo*
Palus: fen
Pan-pipes: *fistula*
Parthenope: Naples
Patior: let
Peace: *pax*
Penelope's father: Icarius
Philosophers, stern: Stoics
Pig: *sus*
Pilleum: cap
Pint: *sextarius*
Pix: pitch, tar
Place next to: *adpono*
Place: *locus*
Plague: *lues*
Planted: *satus*
Plate: *lanx*
Play: *ludo*
Plough: *aro*
Plough: *temo*
Potestas: power
Pray: *oro*

Prayer, entreaty: *votum*: *prex*
Prowl around: *obambulo*
Pudor: shame
Puff up: *sufflo*
Pugio: dagger
Put on: *induo*
Pylos, king of: Nestor
Quadraginta: forty
Quindecim: fifteen
Ransom: *redimo*
Read: *lego*
Rear: *tergum*
Rein: *lorum*
Remain, be left: *resto*
Remus: oar
Repeat: *dicto*
Roast: *torreo*
Rock: *saxum*
Room: *aedes*
Run together: *elido*
Run: *curro*
Rust: *aerugo*
Sacred syllable: *om*
Sand: *arena*
Sappho: Psappho
Scindo: rend, tear
Sea eagle: *erne*
Sea: *mare*
Sea-nymph: Ino, Nereid
Secretly: *clam*
Sedge: *ulva*
Send: *mitto*
Set sail: *vela dare*
Sh!: *st*!
Sharpen: *acuo*
Sheep: *ovis*
Shepherd loved by Galatea: Acis
Shield: *scutum*

Shoulder: *umerus*
Siccus: dry, arid
Sick: *aeger*
Sing: *canto*
Sive, seu: either, or
Six (Greek): *hex*
Sky: *caelum*
Snow: *nivis*
Speak, say: *dico*: *loquor*
Sprout: *enascor*
Stand: *sto*
Stargazer: *astrologus*
Stork: *ciconia*
Suitable: *aptus*
Sun: *sol*
Sunset: *solis occasu*
Swim: *nato*
Sword: *gladius*
Syrian dynast: Seleucid
Tabula: map
Take over illegally: *usurpo*
Tantalus' daughter: Niobe
Teach: *doceo*
Tereus: lover of Philomela
That (of yours): *iste*
Then: *tum*
There: *ibi*: *eo*
Therefore: *ergo*
Thessalian river: Peneus
Thing: *res*
This, these: *hic, haec, hoc*
Threat: *mina*
Three times: *ter*
Through: *per*
Throw back: *reicio*

Thus: *ita, sic*
Tin: *stannum, stagnum*
Tomorrow: *cras*
Too late: *sero*
Touch: *tango*
Tower: *turris*
Tredecim: thirteen
Tree: *arbor*
Tribe, race: *natio*
Triginta: thirty
Troy-builder: Laomedon
Trust: *fido*
Turtle dove: *turtur*
Ulmus: elm
Undecim: eleven
Underworld: Orcus, Dis, Hades

Up-beat: *arsis*
Use: *utor*
V: 5
Venal judge: Bulbus
Viginti: twenty
Violet: iodine
Virgil, birthplace: Mantua
Votum: vow, prayer
Wall: *murus*
Water: *aqua*
Waterfall: *lin*
Wave: *unda*
Well done!: *eu*
Welsh dyke-builder: Offa
Why?: *quam ob rem, cur*
Wife: *uxor*

Wind: *ventus*; south-east: *Eurus*; north: *Boreas*
Wing: *ala*
Winter: *hiems*
Wit: *sal*
With you: *tecum*
Without an age: *sine aetate*
Without lawful issue: *sine legali prole*
Without offspring: *sine prole*
Without: *sine*
Woe: *vae*
Wooden: *ligneus*
X: 10